JOKES, GAGS, TRICKS, GAMES, AND SKILLS FOR EVERY DAD

IAN COUTTS

Published in the USA by Adams Media, an F + W Publications Company
57 Littlefield Street, Avon, MA 02322

Conceived and produced by
Elwin Street Productions
144 Liverpool Road,
London N1 1LA
United Kingdom
www.elwinstreet.com

ISBN-13: 978-1-59869-789-6
ISBN-10: 1-59869-789-7

J I H G F E D C B A

Design by James Lawrence
Illustrations by David Eaton
Printed in Singapore

This publication is designed to provide accurate and authoritative information with regard to the subject matter covered. It is sold with the understanding that the publisher is not engaged in rendering legal, accounting, or other professional advice. If legal advice or other expert assistance is required, the services of a competent professional person should be sought.
—From a Declaration of Principles jointly adopted by a Committee of the American Bar Association and a Committee of Publishers and Associations

This book is available at quantity discounts for bulk purchases. For information, please call 1-800-289-0963.

Visit our home page at www.adamsmedia.com.

Contents

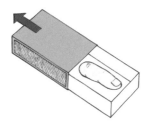

Introduction

Once upon a time, it was all so simple. Dad was the provider. Each morning as the sun came up, he picked up his club and left the cave for another busy day of slaughter. At night he headed home, a freshly killed iguanodon slung over one shoulder. Dad was the protector, too. He watched the mouth of the cave, ready with a fire-hardened pointed stick to take on all comers— mammal, reptile, or Cro-Magnon. And Dad gave you the vital life lessons that made sure you didn't end up as something else's dinner.

But best of all, Dad was fun. After dinner, using the light of the fire, he'd make shadow figures on the wall ("Please, please, Dad," the kids would beg, "do the mammoth again."), or tell jokes and crazy stories ("When I was your age, we dreamed of having an opposable thumb."). Life may have been nasty, brutish, and short but, thanks to Dad, it was also entertaining.

Then somewhere in the ensuing millennia, things started to change. No longer content simply to gather, Mom announced that she wanted to pick up a club, too. No more saber-tooth tigers or rival proto-humans did make protecting the old cave mouth a lot easier—but it also made it rather less important. As for life lessons, in a world of pre-packaged food, who needs to know "Red berries good, green berries bad"?

He may have lost his other roles, and sometimes it feels as if the very idea of Dad himself is under attack, but there remains one place where a father can still shine: Dad as Entertainer. And yet oddly enough, while a father can find any amount of advice regarding his other roles, this essential, unchanging task has been neglected—until now.

Welcome to *Dadzooks*. In the following pages, you'll find the essential lore that every father needs to know. The tricks, jokes, gags, and know-how within these pages are universal classics, passed down over countless generations from man to man. And now, modern Dad, it's your turn. Perhaps as you sit there, picking idly at a fraying thread in that faded Nirvana T-shirt, you think, This isn't for me—I may be a father, but I can't do Dad. You think of those Dads of yore, the kind who built the massive doll houses, the crackerjack soapbox racers. You're a guy who is hopeless with a hammer and a saw. You don't have the proper Dad look: you lack the pipe, the crinkly eyes, the graying temples. I don't even have a cardigan, you tell yourself.

Don't worry. *Dadzooks* requires no great skills and no special tools. You may need one or two accessories—wooden matches, a deck of cards—but in general you won't need to buy anything special. All you really need is a mind relatively free of clutter and a willingness to learn. And part of the fun with the various tricks, jokes, and ideas in *Dadzooks* is that, not only can you learn them and perform them, but, because they are fairly simple, you can teach them to your kids. And some day they can show them to their own kids. The circle of life, as they say, continues.

So follow the instructions, study the diagrams, and commit what you see here to memory and you will become—to your own children at least—the master of magic, the king of comedy, the very fount of family fun.

CHAPTER 1

JOKES, PRANKS, AND GAGS

The proffered finger

Dadzooks 101: the basic tool in any Dad's entertainment kit.

DEGREE OF DIFFICULTY
★★★★★

Scarcely worthy of comment.

APPARATUS

None.

How to

From Archimedes' lever to Descartes' "I think, therefore I am" to Einstein's $E=mc^2$, all revolutions in human knowledge began from the simplest steps. Being an entertaining Dad is no different. This is the fundamental Dad trick, from which all others flow. Here is how it works—but note that this is for use only with the very young. Upon catching your child's attention, offer them your index finger. They will grasp it, delighted. When they let go, offer it to them again. They will grasp it, delighted. Repeat. Not simply entertaining, with this gesture, you are telegraphing a message: Dad is fun.

 Tip: *Remember, a good entertainer knows when to retire an act. The proffered finger works best with those whose age is numbered in months, not years. Unless you plan to add a few wrinkles (the inappropriate breaking of wind when the finger is pulled upon, for example), this is a joke that an older audience will find dull, if not insulting.*

Peek-a-boo

Through the clever use of his hands,
Dad appears and disappears.

DEGREE OF DIFFICULTY
★★★★★

APPARATUS

None.

How to

Here's another one for the very young—simple yet highly popular. First, fix your baby with a steady gaze to gain their attention. Now bring up your hands

to cover your face, then open them like a set of double doors, revealing a beaming Dad. Close them and after the briefest of pauses, open again. Your baby's merriment will know no bounds.

Tip: *You may be surprised by how long a very junior member of your family will find this amusing. Indeed, after but a few short minutes, you may find your enthusiasm lagging considerably faster than theirs. In this case, it may be useful to rely on the "hand-off" maneuver. Picking up the child, you turn and hand them off to their mother.*

Oops-a-daisy

With a little help from Dad, your child slips the surly bonds of Earth.

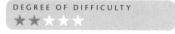
DEGREE OF DIFFICULTY
★★☆☆☆

APPARATUS
None.

How to

In terms of technique, this trick pretty much defines simplicity. Here's how it works: Taking the child in your arms, hold them up in front of your face. Then, with a fluid movement, toss them in the air, while calling out words of cheerful encouragement.

It's all pretty straightforward, but this is one bit of fun that comes with a major caveat: you need to gauge your audience carefully. Is yours an excitable or nervous child? There are those on whom such an airborne excursion, undertaken involuntarily at an early age, has left its mark. Such individuals, even well into advanced middle age, often find themselves unaccountably upset when called upon to use elevators or embark on an aircraft.

Tip: *It seems perfectly self-evident, but it probably can't be said enough—don't drop them. If you are even a little bit uncertain about your skill with this one, just move on. You needn't learn every entertainment in the book.*

Put here there

A selection of novelty handshakes designed to appeal to the younger set.

DEGREE OF DIFFICULTY
★★☆☆☆

APPARATUS

None.

How to

Here is a series of amusing variations on the conventional handshake.

1. Grasping the hand firmly, squeeze it rhythmically while announcing, "I am Dr. Smith, the eminent heart surgeon."

2. Grasping the index and middle fingers in one hand and the ring and little fingers in the other, announce, while pulling on them in turn, "I am Mr. Smith of the Dairy Board."

3. Here's one that owes more than a little to the great Harpo Marx. "Let's shake," you say, and when your unsuspecting interlocutor extends their hand, raise your leg, and drop it into their hand, so that their hand rests just behind the knee. Laughs all round.

Tip: *The lifetime of this trick can be greatly extended by mixing and matching a different shake for every occasion.*

Detachable finger

Simple perhaps, but a timeless classic, and one of the fundamental building blocks in any Dad-as-entertainer's repertoire.

DEGREE OF DIFFICULTY
★★★★★

APPARATUS

None.

How to

Bend your thumb inward and fold the index finger over it to cover its knuckle completely. On your other hand, curl your index finger back. Tuck the stub of this finger under the index finger that's holding back the thumb on the first hand. It should look like the finger is passing behind the index finger and emerging on the other side.

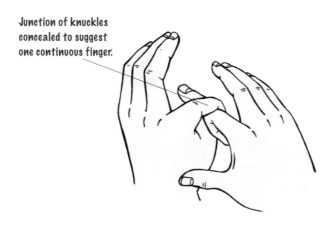

Junction of knuckles concealed to suggest one continuous finger.

Now, assuming a suitable pretext, call your children's attention to yourself—"Hey, look" works well. Then pull back the left hand, giving the impression that you have pulled off the top of your index finger. Bask in the general hilarity.

Movement of left hand simulates severing of upper joint of finger.

"Stump" remains behind, miraculously unbloodied.

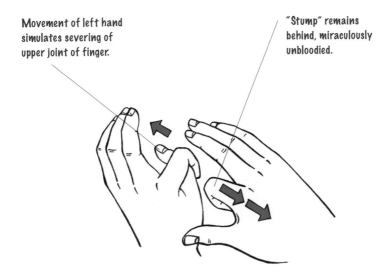

Tip: *This is a simple trick, but not foolproof. Do practice in a mirror beforehand. As a bonus, if you so wish, you can substitute a thumb for the severed index finger, although even the most credulous children are unlikely to be fooled anew by the simple substitution of one finger for another.*

"What's this nose, then?"

Dad magically steals—and then restores—his child's olfactory organ.

DEGREE OF DIFFICULTY
★☆☆☆☆

APPARATUS

None.

How to

A favorite of the older set, this is nonetheless well worth learning as a starter jest for any dad who wishes to entertain his children.

This is really a variation on the finger-removal trick, but practiced on another person—faking removing your own nose would take some doing. Announce to your audience that you can pull their nose off. Reach up and hold the nose between index and middle knuckles of one hand, and give it a slight pinch. As you withdraw your hand, tuck the tip of your thumb in between the curled-over first and second fingers, so that the protruding end resembles the tip of the nose, miraculously and hilariously removed. A jest almost Zen-like in its purity.

Tip: *In theory almost impossible to mess up, but be sure nonetheless to show only the tip of your thumb. Even very young children will grow quickly skeptical if their nose appears to have grown a nail.*

Invisible escalator

Dad rides into the hearts of his children on an imaginary mechanical staircase.

DEGREE OF DIFFICULTY

★☆☆☆☆

APPARATUS

A bench or other form of "cover." Strong thighs are an asset, too.

How to

The bench in question should be above waist height, and have an opaque back rest. A good-sized couch is an adequate replacement, as are a smallish hedge or waist-high fence, for Dads prepared to perform out of doors.

Standing on one side of the bench, with his audience on the other, Dad suddenly announces, "I'm going to the cellar. Can I get you anything?" With that, Dad turns sideways and, while keeping his body as upright as possible, begins to walk forward, slowly bending his legs so that, from the other side of the bench, he appears to ride down, down, down on the escalator.

Tip: *A winner even when unembellished, this visual gag attains classic proportions when combined with proper escalator behavior—staring straight ahead with a bored look, or a furtive glance at the wristwatch.*

Wooden head

Dad raps for good luck, producing a range of percussive effects from the human head.

DEGREE OF DIFFICULTY

APPARATUS
None.

How to

Another one for the more junior set. Place your tongue firmly against your palate, then pull it away, producing a clicking or knocking sound. Practice this until it becomes second nature—this will avoid the embarrassment of "firing blanks."

Now, while casually talking to one or more of your children, shape the hand as if preparing to rap on a door, then quickly, in the words of the old Tony Orlando song, knock three times, on their or your head—with an appropriately light touch if the child's head is receiving the knocks—while simultaneously making your tongue-knocking noise. Dadzooks magic.

Tip: *You might want to mix up your pitches, as they say. If a wooden table or similar surface is available, then you can rap on this with your other hand while simultaneously knocking on the noggin. Either way, it's a winner.*

Ear scratch

Dad takes the advice of Jim Morrison and breaks on through to the other side.

APPARATUS

None.

How to

Another in the battery of finger jokes. Its inherent hilarity is enhanced by the transgressive frisson gained from the implication that Dad's head is, in fact, empty.

Lifting your hand to your ear as if to scratch inside, curl your index finger under so that it looks as if you have inserted it into the ear. Then, planting your tongue firmly in the opposite cheek, move your tongue up and down in concert with the movement of the knuckle in the ear. Voilà! Dad has poked all the way through.

 Tip: *Dads with a low degree of body awareness are encouraged to rehearse in front of a mirror.*

Dad's pet flea

Pa's tiny pal entertains the kids—and meets a sticky end.

DEGREE OF DIFFICULTY
★★☆☆☆

APPARATUS

None, save a straight face.

How to

Announce that you have a trained flea. Carefully remove him from his "house" (a matchbox), holding him gingerly between thumb and forefinger. Place him in your open palm and put him through his paces. Have him jump from hand to hand, one hand moving up as he jumps off, the other dipping slightly as he lands. He might cross a tightrope stretched between the index fingers of each hand—don't forget appropriate circus music—or run up one sleeve and down the other, while you scratch and wiggle frantically. Finally, your flea attempts a triple somersault. Give a drum roll and watch astounded as he loops three times. Ta-dah!

   Hold him out to the audience. "A big hand!" you cry and then start to applaud wildly yourself . . . a look of horror spreading across your face as you realize that you have crushed your star performer.

Tip: *Always keep your eye firmly fixed upon your tiny pal. The better you do that, the more real he is.*

Speaking with tongues

One napkin, one dad, one tongue—an all-time comedy classic.

DEGREE OF DIFFICULTY

★☆☆☆☆

If you're alive you should be able to do it.

APPARATUS

A paper napkin.

How to

We don't know why this is so funny. It may have to do with the fact that the tongue is just one of those inherently funny body parts.

1. Take the paper napkin.

2. Open it, and hold it up over your face.

3. Now stick out your tongue so that it pops through the napkin.

4. Bask in the appreciation.

Tip: *This trick involves making a choice about your role as Dad. Are you entertainer or old school paterfamilias? Talking to your children about politics or what university they should attend may prove arduous if their dominant mental image of you is of a disembodied tongue emerging from a paper napkin.*

Neck crack

Dad attempts a vigorous—and noisy—cure for a crick in his neck.

DEGREE OF DIFFICULTY
★★★☆☆

APPARATUS

One fragile plastic glass, of the sort commonly used to serve drinks on airplanes.

How to

Intended to lighten the tedium of long flights, this trick can also safely be practiced at home. A simple prop gives it a cartoon-like hilarity.

Concealing the plastic cup under his right arm (having first drained its contents), Dad announces that his uncomfortable airline seat has given him a crick in his neck.

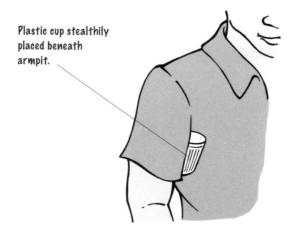

Plastic cup stealthily placed beneath armpit.

Grabbing the top of his head with his left hand, and his chin with his right, he twists his head in the direction of the arm holding the plastic cup, squeezing down hard on it. A hideous crack seemingly emanates from his neck to the untrammeled delight of his audience.

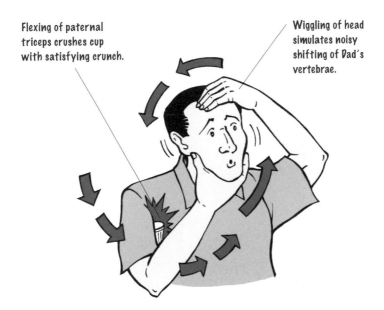

Flexing of paternal triceps crushes cup with satisfying crunch.

Wiggling of head simulates noisy shifting of Dad's vertebrae.

Tip: *Care should be taken to not twist the head too far, risking permanent injury merely for the sake of heightened mirth.*

Severed finger in a box

The addition of a simple prop to the detachable finger joke ensures further hilarity.

DEGREE OF DIFFICULTY
★★★☆☆

APPARATUS

Finger (attached), matchbox.

How to

Take a matchbox or other similar small box (one with a removable lid would work well). Cut a small index finger–shaped hole in the bottom.

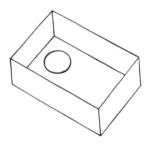 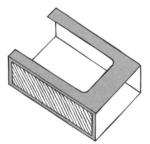

Then, if you are using a matchbox, carefully cut a U-shaped section out of the outer box or sleeve that ends at the edge. You'll see why in a moment.

Slip your index finger through the hole, up to the second joint, bend it down and then slide on the outer portion of the box so that the end of the U rests against the back of the finger. The finger will now be completely hidden inside the matchbox. Call out, "Hey, kids, you'll never believe what I found!" As your youthful audience gathers around you in eager anticipation, slide open the matchbox to display a seemingly severed digit.

For added excitement, encourage your kids to peer excitedly into the box, so their noses almost touch the finger, then give it a sudden twitch. (Earplugs are recommended for this variation.)

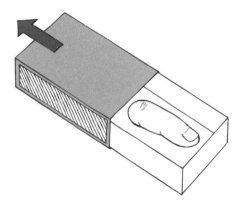

Tip: *The effect can be further heightened by putting a small bed of cotton wool in the bottom of the matchbox to hide the hole. A small dab of ketchup or red dye near the first joint of the finger will work wonders, too. For the utmost hilarity try coloring the finger with a black or blue felt-tip pen.*

Jaws: The father

At the beach or swimming-pool, Dad takes on the role of terror of the deep.

DEGREE OF DIFFICULTY
★ ★ ☆ ☆ ☆

APPARATUS
A fair-sized body of water.

How to

Dad submerges himself in water deep enough for concealment but shallow enough that he can still touch bottom. He then places his right hand on his left shoulder and left hand on his right shoulder, creating the "jaws" of the great white shark. Pushing off from the bottom, he blasts out of the water, snapping his crossed arms to simulate the rapacious frenzy of this deadliest of sea predators.

Tip: *Fathers will find that this move is especially effective if combined with the "Dung-dung, dung-dung, dung-dung" Jaws theme, sung or simply chanted loudly while attacking.*

Coin on the forehead

A beautiful synthesis of practical joke and intelligence test.

DEGREE OF DIFFICULTY
★ ☆ ☆ ☆ ☆

APPARATUS

A smallish coin.

How to

Here's one place where coin-palming skills (see page 50), while not essential, might come in useful. Here's how it works: Holding up the coin, inform your subject that you are going to press the coin hard against their forehead so it will stick there. Then tell them you want them to get the coin loose, but without using their hands.

Take the coin between thumb and forefinger, as if you were about to press it into place. But rather than doing so, simply press with your thumb and palm the coin. The pressure will give your audience the false sensation that there is indeed a coin stuck to their head. From here, the work is theirs.

 Tip: *How long you should let them struggle is an open question. Certainly before they go away to university, you might want to reveal the coin in your hand or have them look in a mirror. A nice treat might be to give them the coin, too.*

Invisibility ray

Dad the magician makes kids disappear—and reappear after a suitable interval.

DEGREE OF DIFFICULTY
★★☆☆☆

APPARATUS

A hand-cranked egg beater (optional), although any plausible invisibility bestower—wand, magic ring, TV remote control—will do.

How to

Works best on a solo child of credulous nature. Announce that you have invented a way to make children invisible. Taking the egg beater, crank the handle while pointing it at the child and tell them you are making them invisible. Suddenly look around, confused. Combining a tone of wonder with slight worry, repeat their name. When they answer, look around frantically. Check under tables and behind curtains. Where the hell is that voice coming from? Begin to feel around for the vanished child clumsily, running your fingers over their face, mussing their hair, and so on. Really make sure that this invisible lump is them. Then crank the handle again until the vanished child reappears.

Tip: *In fiction, invisibility seems to drive its subjects mad— think Claude Rains in* The Invisible Man *or Gollum in* The Lord of the Rings. *A child with the illusion of invisibility may be hard to handle, so be prepared to bring them back fast.*

I, face grabber

Dad, betrayed by his own body, is forced into a life-or-death struggle with his own hand.

DEGREE OF DIFFICULTY

APPARATUS

A set of hands.

How to

Essentially another variant on our "silly daddy" routines. In this, Dad's hand has taken on a life of its own. Suddenly, one hand is attempting to grab onto your face. Astonished, you quickly grab its wrist with your other hand, and attempt to fight it off. It's a superhuman struggle, though, and occasionally, the bad hand gets the upper, uh, hand, and grabs the face, where it knocks glasses askew, musses hair, and pokes fingers into nostrils with hilarious effect. It may even go for the throat, occasioning choking and popped eyes. You fight it off, but each time, it counterattacks.

Tip: *Some, perhaps as a result of unresolved personal issues, worry that they may grow overly enthusiastic. Do not fret; you will not choke yourself unconscious. Nor, unlike other forms of rough play, is it here necessary to have an agreed upon "safe word" ("frogurt," for example) to use should you feel things are going too far.*

Toulouse Lau Dad

France's legendary painter and boulevardier visits the family home.

DEGREE OF DIFFICULTY

Knees may hurt.

APPARATUS

Shoes.

How to

Named, as astute Dads will have guessed, after the diminutive artist Toulouse Lautrec, this trick reaps benefits far beyond the actual effort required on the part of the Dad. Follow these simple steps to become a Dad of Diminished Stature:

1. Take a pair of shoes. Place them in front of you, and then kneel so that your knees are resting on the shoes.

2. If you can work it, try moving forward with a shuffle, so that you appear to actually be walking.

We don't know why, but the basics really are that simple. Kids being, on the whole, untroubled by the niceties of political correctness, once you are down there and moving around, almost everything else you do or say will instantly and magically be hilarious. There is a chance that you will do irreparable damage to the heels of your shoes, but this is surely a small price to pay in pursuit of your art.

This is one little piece of business that works well with additional embroidery. Put on a business suit and shuffle about, and it becomes even funnier. Add a drawn-on beard, glasses, and a bowler (the full Toulouse), and it really takes off . . .

Shoes at knee height simulate comically shortened legs.

The silly hat and drawn-on beard technically render this a "semi-Toulouse."

 Tip: *Beware of going too far: references to José Ferrer or Moulin Rouge are lost on many children.*

CHAPTER 2

MAGIC

Pick a card

A basic card trick that will impress any audience, even adults.

DEGREE OF DIFFICULTY

★ ★ ★ ☆

APPARATUS

A full deck of cards.

How to

You hold in your hand a deck of cards. Fan them out, shuffle them, fire them from one hand to the other, whatever. Ask a member of the audience to take a card. Have them look at it, and tell them to make sure that you don't see it. Have them show it to the other members of the audience. Then tell them to put it back on the top of the deck. Cut the cards once, maybe even a couple of times, pass your hands over the deck in a mysterious fashion, say some appropriate magic words, and then turn the cards over so you can see their faces, and fan them out. Then pull out their card and show it to them.

This classic card trick is really quite simple. The secret lies in what magicians call the key card. At some point—before you begin the trick, while you are performing your preliminary mumbo jumbo, or as you are holding the cards out to your volunteer—sneak a look at the bottom card. This will be your key card. You don't have to be too discreet about sneaking a peek, especially if you can distract your audience at the same time. When you cut the cards, your key card will end up on top of their card. When you flip the cards over, their card will be to

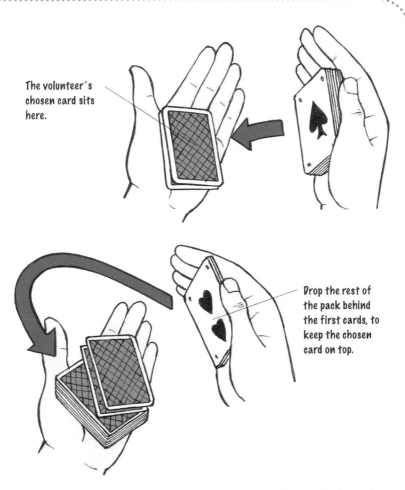

The volunteer's chosen card sits here.

Drop the rest of the pack behind the first cards, to keep the chosen card on top.

the left of your key card. Once you spot it, you know which card is theirs.

The key card need not always be the bottom card. The top card will work just as well—just remember their card will come after it when you fan them out, not before. And once you gain a bit of practice you can even try cutting the cards a couple of times—but be careful—or employing the Hindu shuffle. Here is

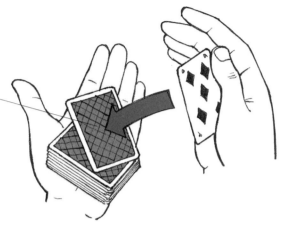

Put the last few cards on top of the pack, so that your key card is next to the chosen card.

how this shuffle works. Once your volunteer has put their card on top of the deck, you pick up the pack in your right hand, and drop the top few cards into your left hand. Then you begin to shuffle by dropping more small packets of cards into your left hand—but always behind the first cards you dropped in there. This goes on until there are only a few cards left in your right hand, including your key card. This packet you drop in front of all the other cards in your left hand. The key card is now on top of their pick. Turn the cards over, work your way through, find your key card and lift out their card—the one on its left.

Tip: *Work at this one solo for a while before debuting it: finding your key card, picking a card out, returning it, and making sure you can find it. When it comes to performing, create some distracting stage patter, to give you a better chance of seeing your key card unobtrusively.*

Starmaker

Here's an ingenious, yet safe way for Dad to play with matches.

DEGREE OF DIFFICULTY
★★★★★

APPARATUS

Four wooden matches and an eyedropper (but you can get by without one).

How to

We have no idea why this works, but it is a neat little bit of magic that is easy to do at home. Take four wooden matches and break each one in the middle, but not completely in two, and then bend them so the two halves are at right angles. Place all four matches together so that they form a cross. Now, carefully place a drop of water on the center of this cross as shown in the diagram. The matches will start to swell. A star is born.

Tip: *Take care to crack all of the matches in about the same place. This trick works best on a Formica-topped table or counter, or some other smooth surface.*

Really nifty match trick

Another trick using matches, virtually impossible to the uninitiated.

DEGREE OF DIFFICULTY
★★★★★

APPARATUS

24 matches, toothpicks, or other small, uniform, skinny sticks.

How to

You want to create a grid of nine squares, three matches wide by three matches deep, using a total of 24 matches. The challenge here for your audience is to leave just two squares by removing eight matches.

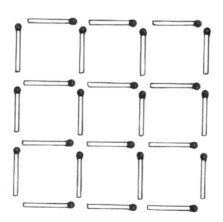

The initial setup, guaranteed to confuse all comers.

The trick here, if it can be called that, is to not get drawn into the idea that the remaining two squares need be the size of the original squares or that they must be side by side.

Here's how it works. Leave all the matches that form the outside of the square where they are. From the top row, take the two inner vertical matches and the two outer horizontal matches. Repeat this in the bottom row. Do nothing to the middle row. Voilà, two squares, one inside the other.

Sly Dad removes these sticks to complete the challenge.

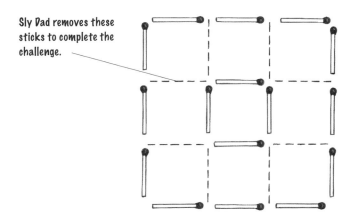

Tip: *Excessively literal-minded children may complain that "Dad cheated." Hear these claims, and respect them. Do not order the plaintiffs to their rooms.*

Number-oh, the mind reader

The mind-reading Dad successfully guesses any number between one and 10.

DEGREE OF DIFFICULTY
★ ★ ★ ☆ ☆

APPARATUS

None, although a certain minimal degree of mental acuity can be helpful.

How to

Here's a simple but foolproof way to convince any child—with the possible exception of a cynical mathematical prodigy—that Dad is a mentalist.

"I am Number-oh, the mind reader," you announce to your audience, in a suitably portentous voice. "I want you to think of a number between one and 10. But don't tell me what it is."

With the number securely recorded in your audience's mind, you then ask them to put it through the following contortions, without telling you any of the results.

1. Multiply the number by three.

2. Add one to the result.

3. Multiply that number by three.

4. Now add the original number.

A pen and paper, or electronic calculator may be required for younger, or less mathematically gifted children. With these four steps completed, you ask them for the result of their calculation. All being well, this should be a double-digit number. You simply need to strike off the second digit and you will be left with the original number.

This is a variant on the trick that many "mind readers" use to figure out a person's age. We have modified it somewhat here. Firstly, for the good reason that you really ought to know your children's ages already, so they are unlikely to be terribly impressed if you manage to guess them. Secondly, if you are the sort of father who needs a trick to learn how old his children are, then you are probably not the sort of father who spends a great deal of time entertaining them in the first place. If indeed you even know where they are. Again, this is a trick that you can explain to the kids once you have performed it—although caution them that, should they try it on their grandparents, they may find that their audience has forgotten the beginning by the time they get to the end.

Tip: As a rule, this is one that works better with older kids (10 and above), who have a firmer grasp of the basics of arithmetic—always assuming that they do not attend a school where arithmetic is not taught, so as to foster their "creativity."

Coin in a bottle

Dad once again puts the mysterious effect of water on matches to good use.

DEGREE OF DIFFICULTY
★★☆☆☆

APPARATUS

A small coin, a bottle, a match, and some water.

How to

This is a variant on the "Starmaker" trick (see page 39), which depends on the interesting effect of water on broken matches.

1. Cracking a match—so that it folds back on itself but the two halves do not separate—place it across the mouth of the bottle with the two ends and the broken "corner" forming a rough triangle.

2. Balance the coin on top of the match triangle. (Make sure it is smaller than the mouth of the bottle—a coin physically too big to pass through the bottle's neck represents a challenge beyond the scope of this book.)

Here is the challenge for the audience: can they get the coin into the bottle without touching the coin, the match, or the bottle? Invite them to try anything they can think of. Blowing is a common tactic, but usually results in coin and match rolling across the floor. Using another matchstick to poke at the coin is ingenious, but should be disqualified on a technicality.

When, barring a miracle or access to this book, your audience gives up, show them how it is done. (Try not to look too smug at the beautiful simplicity of what you are about to accomplish.)

Take a little bit of water (an eyedropper would be useful here, but is not essential) and drip it on to the corner of the matchstick where the broken halves join. The match will straighten of its own accord, and the coin will fall through the gap between the broken halves and drop neatly into the bottle.

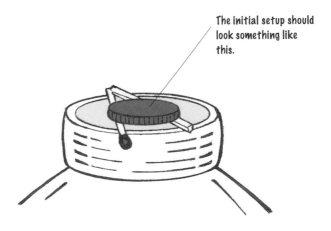

The initial setup should look something like this.

Tip: *Prior practice is probably a good idea.*

Stringing them along

Using the same string as in Cat's Cradle, this very old trick seems to do the impossible.

DEGREE OF DIFFICULTY
★★★★☆

APPARATUS

A string loop, three feet (90 cm) in length.

How to

Calling on a young volunteer from the audience, you ask them for the loan of their forefinger. All they need to do is to hold it up and keep it in place, and you will do the rest. First, loop the string clockwise once around their finger—it must be clockwise for the trick to work (see figure 1). Then pull the two lines toward you. Place your left index finger across the top of the two strings, and loop them back over it, so that the string lies across itself and

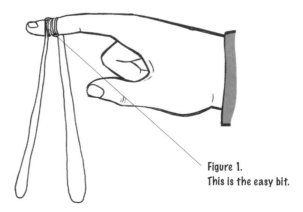

Figure 1.
This is the easy bit.

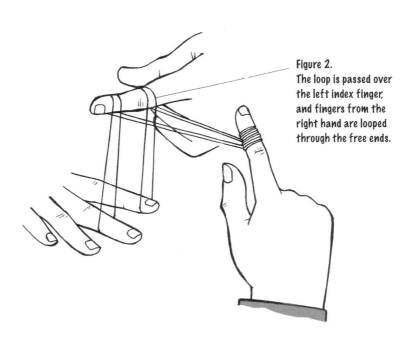

Figure 2.
The loop is passed over the left index finger, and fingers from the right hand are looped through the free ends.

there are two loops hanging down on each side. Bringing up your right hand underneath, stick your index finger through the left loop and your middle finger through the other (see figure 2). Now you want to reverse the right-hand loop on your index finger. To do this, you let it slip off onto your middle finger (and you'll notice that it turns around as you let it off) and then slip it back on to the index finger. If you have done this properly, the inner line of the right-hand loop will now run over your finger and the outer line will emerge from under it. This will be the opposite of the left-hand loop.

Now it gets tricky. Holding your right hand in place, move your left hand up and toward your volunteer's finger. Keep the two loops crooked onto the first joint of this finger. Your goal is to slip these two loops onto their finger. But you aren't going to just drop them on. Instead, you will go past their finger a little, and pivot so that your finger, still with its loops, is, like theirs, pointing upward. You then hook the strings onto their finger (see figure 3).

Finally, you perform the *coup de grâce*. Let the loop off your forefinger, and, using your left hand, pull on the loop held by your middle finger. Rarely do the words "as if by magic" mean so much. The string will unwind, and slide right off the finger around which it was looped.

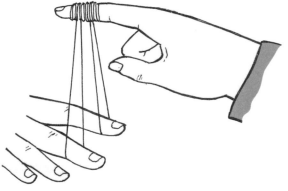

Figure 3.
The loops from your left index finger are transferred to the finger of your patient volunteer.

Tip: *This is a trick where every step must be done exactly right. Otherwise, the end result is a slip knot firmly attached to your victim's index finger. Break down each part and try it several times. And whatever you do, don't despair. It can be done.*

Cork eater

Dad exercises odd-ball dietary habits with the help of one of history's greatest magicians.

DEGREE OF DIFFICULTY
★★★☆☆

APPARATUS

A bowl and several corks.

How to

This is a trick attributed to the great Jean Eugène Robert-Houdin, the man often regarded as the father of modern stage magic. This is one that is probably best done after a big party (a big adult party) when you have a ready supply of corks.

To perform this trick you must be able to palm a cork. This is actually quite simple. You hold the cork with your thumb against your second and third fingers. Raise it to your mouth, open your mouth, then subtly slide the cork down into your palm, where you hold it by squeezing in on its ends slightly, moving in your thumb a little if you have to. Having swallowed the first cork, reach down with the "empty" hand. Drop in the palmed cork with the rest, pick up another and eat it, to general astonishment.

Tip: *Cork palming requires practice to be convincing. The fact that the cork is big makes it fairly easy to palm, but you have to work hard to make sure your hand looks plausibly empty.*

Coin palming

A magic fundamental that will let you extract money from children.

DEGREE OF DIFFICULTY
★★★★☆

APPARATUS

A good-sized coin.

How to

Palming is one of those basics of magic, a foundation for many other magic tricks. We'll give you the basis and suggest a classic move that will let you use your palming skills. And from there you can go where it leads you.

The first step to palming is making sure to pick the right coin. Pennies (of generally any international currency) are too small; so too are American nickels and dimes, and British pound coins.

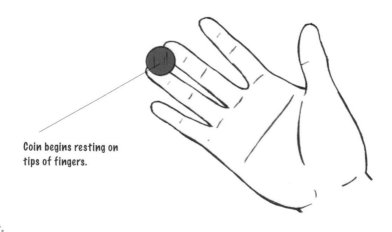

Coin begins resting on
tips of fingers.

Probably the best learning coin would be one that is about an inch (2.5 cm) in diameter. You'll see why the diameter matters in a minute.

Hold the coin in your hand, resting it on the tips of the middle and ring fingers. To palm it means just that, moving it back into the palm. This you can achieve by moving all your fingers back as if making a fist and then letting the coin drop into your palm.

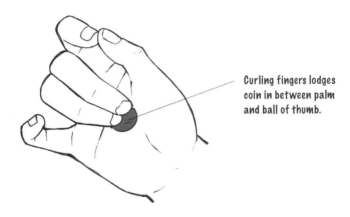

Curling fingers lodges coin in between palm and ball of thumb.

Tip: *Again, the essence of palming is practice. Practice getting the coin into your palm, holding it there, and getting it out again. Once you get good with one coin, you can try stacking two or three in your palm, and pulling them one after the other from a delighted child's ear.*

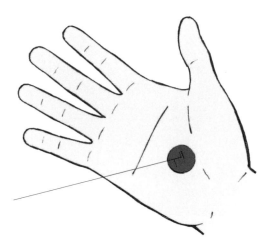

The coin stays here until its miraculous reappearance.

Once there, grasp the coin between the pad on the outside of your palm and the fleshy area under your thumb. By pressing in with your thumb you can hold it quite securely. This is why you need the right-sized coin—too small and you won't be able to keep a grip. Practice this one a lot and in front of the mirror. You want this to look natural to your audience.

As we said, palming is a basic of many tricks, and once you get good at it, you'll think of all sorts of ways to use it. But let's focus on a proven winner in the repertoire of fatherly fun: pulling coins from ears. Here's how you do it. First, stealthily palm a coin into your hand. Then, looking at your child, subtly set up the trick. "Wait!" you exclaim. "What's that? Why it's . . ." and at this point you palm the coin in reverse—loosening your thumb control to let the coin drop onto your middle and ring fingers, guided by your thumb. It'll look like you're pulling it from their ear.

Two corks

A baffling—but fun—trick to perform with two corks.

DEGREE OF DIFFICULTY
★ ★ ★ ☆ ☆

APPARATUS

Two corks.

How to

While we are on the subject of sleight of hand, this is a neat little illusion that the father of the author of *Dadzooks* used to do.

You take two corks, and tuck one in between the thumb and forefinger of each hand, holding them tight. Announce that you are going to grab each cork in the opposite hand and remove it, and show that to do so directly means they bump together. Now, keeping the corks firmly in place, twist your left hand around, and plant each thumb firmly in the palm of the opposite hand. Then you shift your thumb and put it over the end of the cork nearest the palm and slide the forefinger over the opposite end of the cork. Hey, presto, the two corks come away.

Tip: *It can take a little while to work out how this can be achieved. Our advice is to be patient and trust the magic. (And to practice in private before attempting a performance.)*

Two-card trick

A neat bit of presto-chango that puts business cards to actual use.

DEGREE OF DIFFICULTY
★★★☆☆

APPARATUS

A coin, a paper bag (a small gift bag works well), and two business cards.

How to

This trick is typically done using two identical playing cards from two separate card decks. Here, we substitute business cards simply because, while not everyone has two decks of cards, a lot of modern adults seem to have thousands more business cards than they could ever possibly give away.

As preparation, place one of the business cards in the bag when your audience isn't looking. (This is a chance to use those palming techniques we talk about on pages 50–52.)

Now draw your audience's attention and begin the trick. Place the bag, a coin, and the second business card on the table. Pick up the bag in one hand. With your other hand, pick up the business card from the table and put it in the bag. Then pick up the coin and drop it into the bag, too.

Now grab the top of the bag with your hand and squeeze it shut. Shake the bag, while intoning some appropriate magical phrases (the "Ah-yeah-yeah-yeah-yeah-yeah-yeah-yeah-yeah-yeah-yeah" bit from "Oops, I Did it Again" works well.) Now open up the bag and say to your audience, "Let's remove the card, shall we?" As you reach in to pick up one of the cards, make sure you grasp the penny along with it. Then, as your hand emerges from the bag, hold the card so that the penny, which you also take out, is hidden behind it. Subtly put the card and the coin into a pocket, all the while keeping the coin out of your audience's view.

All that is required now is an appropriately showy finale. Ask your audience, "What do you think is still in the bag?" When they answer, "The coin," pull out the other card with a flourish.

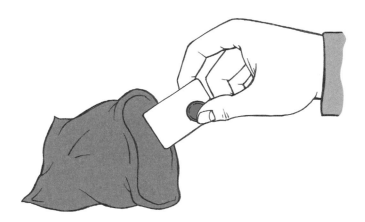

Tip: *The key to this trick is subtle concealment. Your audience shouldn't see the first card go into the pile, and they shouldn't notice the coin coming out. And if they are skeptical, you can offer to do it again—either by palming one card and dropping it in, or by placing one carefully behind the other, so it looks like just one card.*

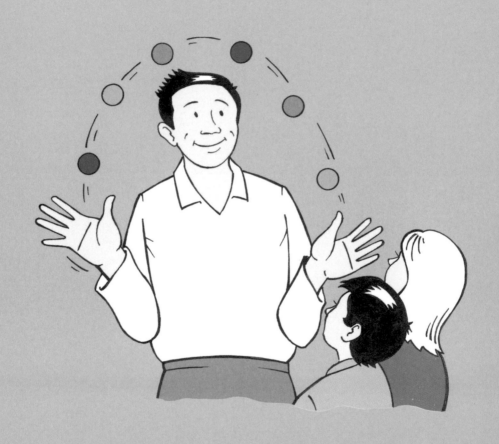

CHAPTER 3

SKILLS AND INGENUITY

Homemade volcano

The awe-inspiring power of nature unleashed in your own kitchen.

APPARATUS
Small plastic bottle cut in half, or similar container; vinegar; liquid dish soap; baking soda; paper towel; glitter; food coloring (optional).

How to

Just how elaborate you want to make this one is up to you. By boosting the proportions of the ingredients used you can take this trick from the homegrown and humble to an eruption of Krakatoa-like proportions. Here, in brief, is how it works:

1. Take your paper towel. Put in it one part baking soda. Add glitter if desired. Fold the towel loosely around the ingredients to make a package.

2. In your container, put one part vinegar and half that amount of liquid dishwashing detergent. To this add food coloring, if you so desire, to make the eruption more dramatic.

3. When your audience is assembled, drop the solid packet of ingredients into the liquid-filled container. A colorful, glittering eruption will result.

The eruption is an open-ended event. Some children will be delighted with the mess all on its own; others will enjoy making it into a performance. If you have the time, the energy, and the skill, you can create a proper mountain for your volcano to erupt out of, either from brown cardboard or papier-mâché (which would let it double as a science project). If you are considering moving your volcano out of doors, you might even heap up dirt around your bottle or container for a more convincing eruption.

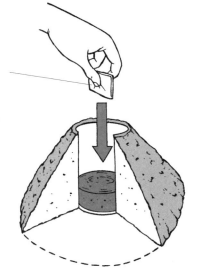

Solid ingredients dropped into plastic container, enclosed in papier-mâché volcano.

Tip: *You can dress up to heighten the drama: for a South Seas feel, fashion sarongs from beach towels for you and your audience. At the moment of eruption, grab their hands and, tearing from the room, proclaim in your finest pidgin, "Him big fella blow top! Quick, quick! We run along path marked Mary!"*

Coat hanger and coin trick

Not a magic trick as such, this is nonetheless mind-boggling.

APPARATUS

One wire coat hanger and one small coin.

How to

First, find a wire coat hanger the tip of whose hook has been cut flat. This may take some doing and you may have to file or sand it down with emery cloth. Then take the coat hanger by the bottom of the loop and, holding on to the hook, pull it, bending the hanger into a diamond shape. You want to balance this diamond on your forefinger, so that it swings loosely like a pendulum, with the hook at the bottom of the diamond. At this point it becomes evident why the tip of the hook must be flat. Take your coin and balance it on this mini plateau. Yes, it is easier to say than to do, but it can be done. This will take several tries, but with care and repetition, you will be able to balance the coin. This is good. Now, moving your finger from side to side, start the hanger (and the coin) swinging back and forth. Impressive, but wait: once you have a rhythm going, you are going to swing the hanger—and the coin—right around. (Note: This will only work if you swing it in the direction of the hook.) Again, yes, this is easier said than done, but it is possible.

By this point, your audience will be impressed. Dad has done the impossible. In fact, no. Dad is about to do the impossible. You are going to stop the hanger spinning, but the coin will stay in place. Stop laughing. Here's how it works. When you want the hanger to stop, extend your arm in front of you, keeping it swinging, then take one large step in the direction in which you are spinning the hanger, and stop turning it. You are no longer Dad; you have attained god-like status.

Balancing the coin here is something of a feat in itself, but persevere.

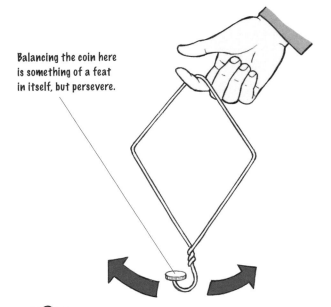

Tip: *The difficulty in performing this trick may discourage many fathers. To be honest, it really can take a very long time to master. Indeed, it might be wiser to see it as not so much a children's amusement than a career choice.*

The fountain of Mentos

Mentos, the world's most popular chewable mint, meet diet cola with an unforgettably messy outcome.

DEGREE OF DIFFICULTY

★☆☆☆☆

(Some caution necessary.)

APPARATUS

One roll of Mentos, one 2-liter container of diet cola, paper tube (optional).

How to

You may not realize it while reading this book, but many of the tricks and skills recorded here have a venerable history. Victorian dads, perhaps even Elizabethan dads, performed some of these very diversions for their children. But fatherhood does not stand still. Here is a neat little trick you can show your kids using two popular modern treats: Mentos, those chewy mints from the Netherlands, and diet cola. Spectacular, it is also educational, providing us with a vivid demonstration of the way in which carbon dioxide, found in all carbonated drinks, can, with the aid of the dissolving sugar coating and gum arabic contained in Mentos, sunder the tight bonds that typically hold water molecules together. Which conclusively proves—uh, something. Here is another activity that might well wait until Mother is elsewhere, or at the very least until her car turns the corner.

Take a bottle of diet cola (diet versions work well and are not terribly sticky, an advantage that will become clear in a moment), open it, and set it down in an open space, ideally outdoors. Make sure that the ground is solid and level so the bottle will not fall over. Next, unwrap all the Mentos. You want to drop them in the carbonated drink. But not one at a time—they need to hit the fluid virtually all at once, which is harder than you might think. One good way to do this is to rig sort of a paper tube to hold them all. Keep the end shut by pinching it with your thumb and forefinger and then hold it over the mouth of the bottle. Release them, stand back, and behold your very own cola-flavored equivalent of the water features of Versailles, Rome's magnificent Trevi fountain, or Las Vegas's fabulous Bellagio Hotel, as a plume of fizzy diet drink rockets skyward.

 Tip: *After dropping the Mentos into the cola, be prepared to run—very, very fast.*

Balloon animals

Rubber zoology that you can share with your kids.

APPARATUS

Bendable balloons, a non-human air source.

How to

In general in this book, we steer clear of entertainments that need any tools or materials you can't find lying around the house. We'd like to make an exception for balloon animals. Here is a *divertissement* that punches far above its weight. Learn this one and you'll be more than a father-entertainer; you'll have attained the status of meta-Dad. That said, the equipment isn't terribly hard to come by. Balloon animals need long, skinny latex balloons available in joke stores, party supply shops, and probably in toy departments elsewhere. (On a green note, they are fully bio-degradable, too.) When you go to buy them, just explain what you need them for. A caution: these balloons are a little heavier than conventional balloons, so unless you have the lungs of a Sherpa raised in the foothills of the Himalayas, you'll need a source of air. This can be an electric pump but a bicycle pump or similar hand pump will work just as well. Just hold the balloon over the nozzle—you don't need that good a seal—and fill 'em up.

There isn't really a secret to creating balloon animals. All you need to know is how to bend the balloon in different directions, using these twists in the balloon to create different shapes. Let's take a look at the dog, the basic balloon animal.

Take one of your balloons and inflate it, leaving about 3 inches (7.5 cm) uninflated at the end—you'll need this slack. Knot the mouth of the balloon. From the knotted end, first measure down roughly 3 inches (7.5 cm) and make a twist in the balloon. What you have here (let's call it a link, like in a sausage), is your dog's head. For the moment, don't let go, because it will unwind. Now measure down a further 3 inches (7.5 cm), and make another twist. That's one of his ears. OK, now fold these two links down, so that they run along the side of the balloon. Now measure off a third link—his other ear—and give it a twist. When you have done this, take your first link, and bend it across the balloon, so that the twist between the first and the second link overlaps the

Twisting two sections together like this is the basis of your creation.

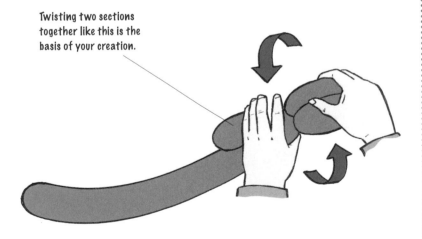

twist between the third link and the rest of the balloon. Twist the first link around this link twice. This is called locking, and it means the twists won't come loose. You now have the dog's head and ears.

Now measure down the balloon another 3 inches (7.5 cm), and make a twist. This is his neck. After this make another twist, followed by another one. These are his front legs. Bend the third link up so it is beside the second link, and twist the last joint around the neck joint, locking it. You now have the neck, the front legs, and a long, unformed body.

Measure off a few more inches and twist to seal off the body link, then make two more twists (are we thinking dachshund or beagle?) as before, creating two more links that will become the rear legs. Fold up at the joint between the legs and twist the last

Repeat further down
to create front legs.

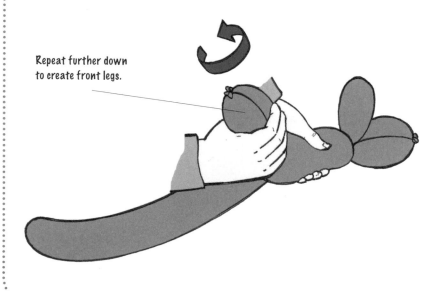

The end of the balloon forms a convenient tail.

joint twice around the hip joint, to make his tail. You have inflatable canine perfection.

Once you get the basics of twisting and locking, you can move on to other animals: the giraffe (make the neck longer), rabbits (boost the ears, and then boost the hind legs and tuck them under the body), and so on. Let your imagination and experimentation be your guide. That said, if you are entertaining at a children's birthday party, it is best to avoid overtly sexual or potentially sacrilegious balloon figures.

Tip: *Avoid rubbing the sides of the balloons excessively when making figures as this can weaken them.*

Weather Dad

You don't need to be a weatherman to know which way the wind blows.

DEGREE OF DIFFICULTY

APPARATUS

None.

How to

This is another one of those great skills, one that will impress—and more importantly, inform—your audience. It is perhaps a tiny simplification, but for the purposes of this trick all our concerns about the weather will be reduced to one question: Is it going to rain, or, if it is cold, is it going to snow?

The simplest way to answer this question is to look at the clouds. If you see only very high clouds, those wispy cirrus clouds, then it probably won't rain anytime soon. If the clouds you are looking at are altostratus or altocumulus—what you might think of as the middle management of the cloud world—you can probably expect some precipitation in ten to fifteen hours. Those big, fluffy central casting–style clouds, the cumulus clouds, generally mean good weather, as long as there isn't much vertical build-up. That is typically called a thunderhead, and you'll soon find out why. Be forewarned: If you see these big fluffy guys forming to the northwest and southwest, you may see rain within five to ten hours. The other low clouds to worry about are those solid, low-hung, socked-in clouds—classic rain clouds, in fact.

If a thunderstorm starts, you can demonstrate another skill—telling how far away the lightning is. When you see a flash, start counting. If the lightning is about a mile away, it will take about five seconds for the sound of thunder to reach you. If it's closer, it'll take less. By timing the lapse between the lightning and the thunder, you can tell if a storm is approaching or moving away.

There are a host of folk sayings that go with weather prediction—some nonsense, some reasonably accurate. Here are a few that are generally true:

- "Red sky at night, sailors delight; red sky in morning, sailors take warning." A red sky at night is usually caused by stratocumulus clouds, which generally signal that no rain is likely for the next 20 to 24 hours. A cloudy morning, which creates a red sky, however, suggests that rain is imminent.

- "Mackerel sky and mare's tails make tall ships carry low sails." Mare's tails are the very high, wispy clouds, while a mackerel sky is another high-altitude formation, seen when the clouds are beginning to transform into lower-altitude clouds. Both are signs of high winds.

- Finally here's one that works at least in the northern hemisphere, where the weather moves from west to east: "Beware the bolts from north or west; in south or east the bolts be best." Generally, a thunderstorm to the north or west is heading for you; one to the south or east won't bother you.

As with any mystical performance, presentation can make or break Weather Dad's credibility. A simple "Looks like rain," while pleasingly understated, is unlikely to impress any but the most doting child. Weather Dad might instead sniff the air once or twice, narrow his eyes critically as he scans the horizon, and mutter, "South-east-by-east, let's say 20 or 30 miles per hour . . ." He might then leave a moment's pregnant pause before turning a grim visage to his young charges and darkly warning: "Storm's coming." With such a virtuoso performance to fall back on, a quick look at the weather pages of the day's newspaper, if available, is an excusable alternative to any actual cloud-spotting.

Incidentally, Dad may wish to avoid putting a definite time-frame to his predictions. After all, there's bound to be a storm along eventually . . .

Tip: *Don't feel nervous because you don't really understand all the science behind predicting the weather. Do you think those people you see on TV talking over a bunch of shifting clouds have the faintest idea of what's going on?*

Skipping stones

Dad handily displays his awesome stone-skipping mojo.

DEGREE OF DIFFICULTY
★★★★☆

APPARATUS

A selection of flat stones.

How to

This will brighten any trip to a lake or the seaside. Start with the right stone. Look for a flattish rock that has been worn smooth by the waves—it'll have less resistance, so when it hits it should skip nicely. Hold the stone between thumb and forefinger, resting slightly on the middle finger. We prefer a backhand stroke, throwing across the body, but most aficionados throw sidearm-style, winding back and then letting go, which is good for speed. You want to throw hard, but more importantly, you want to throw more or less parallel to the water, even, if possible, with the stone spinning in a slightly nose-up configuration, so that it hits the water rear-first, which should enhance its skipping potential.

Tip: *You want a calm day for this. Not only so the water is relatively flat, but so that the wind does not interfere with your stone's trajectory. If you're coming off several years' inactivity, your first skips won't be that good. Be patient.*

Dad the tracker

A few simple tips will enable you to create an image of Dad as a skilled woodsman.

DEGREE OF DIFFICULTY
★★★☆☆

APPARATUS

A good pair of eyes.

How to

Identifying animal tracks isn't all that difficult. Typically there are only a few animals whose tracks you are likely to come across in the woods or fields and if you know those, you should be fine.

Deer prints

Deer have a cloven (that is, two-part) hoof, which creates a print that is a sort of split heart shape. Sometimes there are two small dots behind this, left by the dew claws. An adult deer's footprint is typically 2 to 3 inches (5 to 7.5 cm) long.

Dogs, cats, and related animals have a footprint with a central pad and then four distinct toes. One major difference between cats' and dogs' prints, other than size, is that typically in a dog's footprint you can also see the marks left by the claws—unlike cats they can't retract them. Cats' prints are generally about 1 to 1¹/₂ inches (2.5 to 4 cm) across. Other wild cats, lynxes, bob cats, and mountain lions have a footprint very like that of the domestic cat, but bigger.

Cat prints

We spoke of dog-like animals above because there are other creatures in the woods that leave a print like a dog's. Foxes, for example. A fox's footprint is typically 2 inches (5 cm) long and 1$\frac{1}{2}$ inches (3.8 cm) across. Coyotes leave large, dog-like prints that are a bit narrower than a domestic dog's, and show only two claws—on the innermost toes. These claws point inward.

Dog prints

Badgers have a foot that in some ways resembles a dog's, except that the main pad is quite broad and it has five toes, not four. This holds true for all the badger's kin—weasels and fishers, for example. Raccoons, which now survive largely by knocking over trash cans in the suburbs, have feet that almost resemble human hands, albeit with claws. Possums also have hands; in fact, these look uncannily like a child's hands, right down to a human-style opposable thumb.

Members of the rodent family (this includes mice, voles, squirrels, chipmunks, and woodchucks) typically have four toes on the front foot and five on the back. Among rodents, rabbit prints are very distinctive. You'll see two large prints side by side (their rear feet) and then much smaller alternating footprints (their front feet).

When it comes to bird prints, no matter which part of the world you find yourself in, the one thing you can tell is whether the bird that made the prints you're looking at is one that's used to walking on the ground, or one that gets around mostly by flying. Pigeons and starlings are good walkers, and they leave larger footprints that alternate the way ours do. Most smaller birds hop, which means they leave footprints in pairs.

Rabbit prints

Tip: *Avoid simply pointing at the track and saying, "Look, kids, a badger was here." Tracking wants a bit of drama. Consider something like this. Upon seeing a track, or more likely having your kids call it to your attention, drop to one knee. Examine it closely. Squint into the distance. "Hmm. Badger," you say. Poking at it with a stick, you might add, "Fresh, too." Then, gesturing vaguely in front of you, try adding something like, "Headed that way." Finally, go for a suitable capper: "And whereas I see many prints heading into the woods," you say, fixing your young listeners with a steely eye, "I see none coming out."*

Cry of the lawn

Behold a world of noise in a single blade of grass.

DEGREE OF DIFFICULTY
★★☆☆☆

Longish blade of grass.

How to

You'll need a blade of grass about 3 to 4 inches (7.5 to 10 cm) long to do this one. Pick one that is fairly wide. Tension it between the tips of your thumbs and the mound of your palm. There should be a small gap between your thumbs, and the blade of

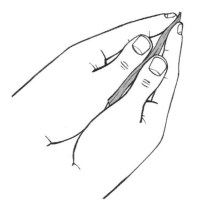

grass should be tight between them. Raise your hands to your lip and blow, producing a high-pitched squawk, caused by the grass acting as a membrane and vibrating.

Tip: *A little extra flesh helps to keep a seal around the grass, so bony-handed Dads might want to eat a few extra doughnuts to help with this one (see pages 96-97).*

Native American sign language

Dad invokes the spirit of the legendary Plains tribes while sitting at the kitchen table.

DEGREE OF DIFFICULTY
★★★★★

APPARATUS
None.

How to

First off, understand that you are not going to be fluent. Developed on the plains of central to western North America to enable disparate groups speaking grammatically unrelated languages to communicate, Native American sign language is incredibly complex, on a par with the sign languages used today by deaf people. What follows will not be enough to let you translate for a group of Oglala Sioux who urgently need to explain to an English-speaking traffic cop why they were parked in a no-stopping zone. What we're going to focus on here are just a few common signs that will amuse and interest your audience.

Most sign speech was made with the hands held at approximately chest level, and usually with the right hand, the left functioning to embellish or modify what the right was saying. Even relatively simple ideas often consisted of one or more symbols used together. Here are a few basic terms:

Father: Cup your right hand slightly, and tap the right side of your chest gently two or three times. This is followed by the sign for man: point the right index finger upward, keeping your other

fingers closed, and with the palm facing the other person.

Mother: Cup your right hand slightly and tap the left-hand side of the chest.

Son: Make the sign for man, then, with the right hand closed and the index finger extended upward, indicate your son's height.

Daughter: Place your hands with the fingers slightly bent on either side of your head, then move your hands downward as if using a comb. This sign can also be made using just the right hand.

Baby: Here's a pretty straightforward one. Clench the right fist and hold it against your front, then cradle the right forearm with the left hand as if holding a baby.

Now that we have those basics in place, let's add a few more complex ideas:

Eat: Cup the right hand and bring it to your mouth, then lower it. Repeat this as if scooping up food.

Drink: Turn your side to the person you are talking to, cup your hand and draw it up slowly to your mouth. This also means water.

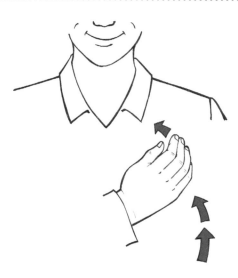

I love you: Sign language uses the symbol for friendship for love, so basically you might try something like first pointing to yourself with your thumb (me), then pointing at the other person with your index finger (you), then finally making the symbol for friendship: the index and middle fingers of the right hand held out together and raised to shoulder level.

Last of all, very crudely transliterated here, a phrase any dad might find useful: First press the nail of your index finger against your extended thumb, then point your right index figure at your child, then your thumb at yourself. Finally tap your left breast with your right hand, creating the sign language version of every Dad's helpful standby: Ask your mother.

Tip: *Further research is recommended before trying these outside the immediate family.*

Spoon on nose

A great time-killer between courses or while waiting to be served.

DEGREE OF DIFFICULTY
★★★☆☆

APPARATUS

A teaspoon.

How to

We know that we shouldn't encourage our kids to play with their food. But to play with implements, ahh, that is a different story. While you'll hear fans of this jolly jest argue the merits of sterling over silver plate, pretty much any teaspoon will do. Here's how it works. First, lick the tip of your finger and rub the end of your nose. Next, breathe on the spoon once or twice so that it fogs up. Take the teaspoon, tilt your head back slightly, and balance the spoon on your nose. Pure mirth. Indeed, never in the history of father-inspired mirth has so much been generated by so little.

Tip: *Pick your spot. Home is always good, and so, in our opinion, is any fancy restaurant where the kids get bored waiting for food. If the waiters don't like it, you know what? Your money is as good as anyone else's. On the other hand, you might want to leave this one at home if attending a state dinner, particularly one where royalty will be present.*

Ventriloquism

"Read my lips" just won't mean the same thing when you can throw your voice.

DEGREE OF DIFFICULTY

APPARATUS

None essential.

How to

While people do spend years getting really good at it, basic ventriloquism is actually surprisingly easy to grasp.

The goal, obviously, is to speak without moving your lips. But this doesn't mean with your mouth shut. The trick is to lock your jaws only slightly open, in a comfortable but unobtrusive fashion with the lips just slightly apart. This will let you speak without appearing to. Because some of the sounds we normally make when we talk require us to move our lips, we'll have to learn how to make these sounds in a slightly different way. The letters that cause the most trouble are B, F, M, P, and V. For B, try substituting a G sound, so that boys become goys and bank, gank. For F breathe hard as you say it and try for a sort of H sound. So Fred becomes Fhred. For M try N or Ng, substitute a K for any Ps (which doesn't sound as odd as you might think), and with a V try breathing out hard as you say it. Above all, practice. Stand in front of the mirror, and run through the alphabet again and again. You don't want to give anything away, so this is best done in the restrooms at work. Repair there three or four times a day and recite the alphabet. Who could possibly mind? Then move on to words.

Of course, once you have gained the ability to throw your voice, you need somewhere, so to speak, to toss it. This need not require anything elaborate. Kettles and pots—anything with a lid, really—can be made to talk by raising and lowering the lid. You can rig a dummy by drawing an eye on both sides of the first joint of your index finger, and putting a nice pair of red lips around the opening created by this finger and your thumb. Wrap a dishtowel or other cloth around your forearm, cradle it in your other arm, and you have a talking baby.

We don't know why, but the malevolent ventriloquist's dummy seems to be a favorite of popular culture. This can be relatively benign—Edgar Bergen's famed Charlie McCarthy, for example. Or, in horror movies, it can be downright evil. You never seem to meet a ventriloquist's dummy that isn't looking for trouble.

Without venturing into the territory covered by the *Chucky* movies and so forth, you can try adding a little edge to your routine. It might start easily enough—the talking baby says it doesn't want to sing "My Favorite Things" from *The Sound of Music.* Try to muffle it (throwing muffled "mmpfs" is a hell of a lot easier than trying to actually speak). Finally, in an echo of "I, face grabber" (see page 31), baby/talking hand can go for the throat. But go easy on this—you have to do its voice, too, and the kids are going to get suspicious if your dummy seems to be choking while *your* throat is being grabbed.

Or you can use a human volunteer. Hoisting a child on to your knees, announce that you are going to make them talk. Whenever you tap them on the back, they open and shut their mouth, while you make the words come out of them. Any shortcomings in skill will be overlooked in the ensuing heightened hilarity.

Tip: *When using a child as your dummy, it is best to resist the temptation to make them say what you want to hear. Go easy on lines like "I will eat all my vegetables" and "I will never whine at bedtime." This is meant to be their entertainment, not your wish-fulfillment.*

Shadow figures

Through the adroit use of hands and light,
Dad makes shadowy figures come alive.

DEGREE OF DIFFICULTY
★★★★☆

APPARATUS

A light-colored wall and a light source—a desk lamp works best but almost any lamp can be pressed into service.

How to

Before TV there were the movies, and before the movies there were shadow figures or, as they were sometimes called, shadowgraphs. These require some practice but readily repay the practitioner and are often best performed at night, in a child's bedroom, before they go to sleep.

Taking your light source, aim it at a light-colored wall, one where you'll have a marked degree of contrast. Place your hands between the light and the wall, and begin to weave magic. What follows are instructions on how to make three very effective shadowgraphs. With these under your belt, you can move on and create your own. As always, getting good means practice.

The following assume a light on the left, a wall to the right.

The dog

On the right hand, point your thumb upward. This is the dog's ear. Now curl back your index finger (made supple from repeatedly performing the missing finger jokes in Chapter One). Point the other three fingers of the hand straight out, with the middle and ring fingers held together but a small space left

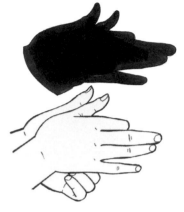

between the ring and baby fingers. Then place the left hand just back a bit from the right, with the thumb held up. This will be the other of the dog's ears. Your fingers should be curled under—just a little, not into a fist. The ring and baby fingers of the left hand should protrude below the right hand, creating the dog's neck. (By altering the position of the ring finger you may, should you wish, give the dog a goiter. You know your audience.)

The rabbit

Once you have mastered the dog, try this more complex figure. With palm down, extend the index and middle fingers of the right hand, slightly bent. Curl the ring and middle fingers loosely under and rest them on the thumb, which is also pointing forward and slightly curved. Rest the left hand on the right hand, palm up, with the thumb held at the side of the hand. The index finger should be crooked, leaving a small space for light to get through (the rabbit's "eye"). The middle finger is extended in a rather unpleasant fashion (perhaps mirroring how you feel about the rabbit at this stage) to form the left ear, and the ring and baby fingers together form the right ear. *Regardez! Un lapin!*

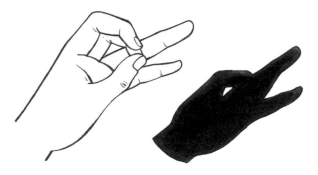

Two ducks

In this shadowgraph, sometimes also called "two baby birds," we attempt not simple lone figures but a tableau.

Holding the thumb in at the side of each hand, curl the index and middle fingers back together and rest the middle finger on your ring finger between the first and second joint. This gives you the head and the eye of your two ducks. Make sure that the ring finger is extended straight out. Next, stick your baby finger out and point it slightly down, so that its tip is about an inch below the ring finger. Together these give the bill of the duck. With two figures, the possibility for true performance exists. Waggle your lower baby finger to make the ducks talk; or, depending on your own theories of child-rearing, even kiss or fight.

Tip: *A world of possibilities lies before the ambitious shadow puppeteer. With persistent practice, progressively more complex and amusing shadowgraphs can be created. What will please your viewers and what is suitable is for you to decide. That said, more sophisticated, complex, and perhaps unsettling images (Angelina Jolie comes to mind) are probably best reserved for older children.*

Kazoo comb

Dad creates musical magic from the mundane.

DEGREE OF DIFFICULTY
★★★★★

APPARATUS

A pocket comb, tissue paper.

How to

Though criminally ignored by most of the world's major orchestras, the kazoo guarantees to generate a buzz. You'll need a small comb and a piece of tissue paper. Please note: when we say tissue we don't mean a Kleenex or "facial tissue" but the thinner and stiffer tissue paper sometimes used to wrap presents. (Actually, a normal piece of paper will just about do the job, but it won't vibrate as nicely.)

Measure a small piece of tissue the width of the comb, and long enough to fold right over it. Fold it over the comb, on the side of the ends of the teeth. (For this reason it is probably desirable not to use a very old comb.) We don't know why but this produces the best vibration. Now carefully put the kazoo comb into your mouth, teeth-side first. You have to do this very gingerly and it really is vital to keep your lips as dry as possible. Hold down on the comb and paper with your lips. Now hum. Any tune you like. The tissue should vibrate, creating a satisfying kazoo sound. Incidentally, do remember to let the kids have a turn—tempting as it is to run all the way through Pink Floyd's "The Wall," they want to learn how to do this themselves.

There are plenty of other instruments in your house. Pots and pans make good drums when played with a wooden spoon (although they can permanently impair your sanity). A paper towel roll can make a trumpet: pucker your lips, press it hard against your mouth, and blow. Ordinary tablespoons work especially well as a percussion instrument. Just take two and hold them bottom to bottom, with your index finger wedged in between, and your thumb pressing down on the handle of the top spoon. Hold the spoons in your right hand, place your left hand palm down over them, and then bang the spoons down on your thigh and up against the palm of your hand. Or hold your palm up, and then sort of drag the spoons across it and across both thighs, producing a tickety-tick-tick percussion effect. (For some reason, the minute you start to play the spoons you will automatically begin singing the "Merry Ploughboy" and other Irish folksongs. Neurologists theorize that the spoons trigger the little-understood "Hibernian gland" buried deep in our brains.)

Tip: *You may be tempted to try the ultimate Dad trick: using your children to make money. If so, be prepared for tradeoffs. If you think your kids don't show much gratitude now . . . Go ahead, rake in the dough, but be prepared to turn on the TV in 20 years' time and see some Hollywood B-lister in a bad rug and tricked-up fake teeth playing you in a tell-all biopic.*

Newspaper palm tree

A tropical delight torn, as the old cliché has it, from today's headlines.

DEGREE OF DIFFICULTY
★★★☆☆

APPARATUS

A newspaper, preferably but not essentially tabloid-sized, and a pair of scissors.

How to

We refer herein to tabloid-sized papers, but a broadside page torn in half would work as well. (We are aware that newspaper formats in many parts of the world have undergone an astounding shrinkage in recent years. If nothing you can get your hands on seems to be either a tabloid or a broadside, just do the best you can.) You might also use one of those widely available community giveaway papers, although those pages advertising discreet daytime encounters with hot she-males are best avoided for the uncomfortable questions they raise.

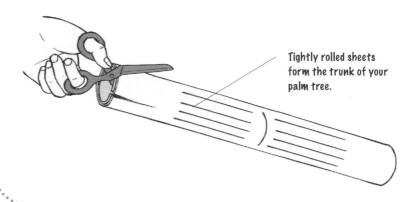

Tightly rolled sheets form the trunk of your palm tree.

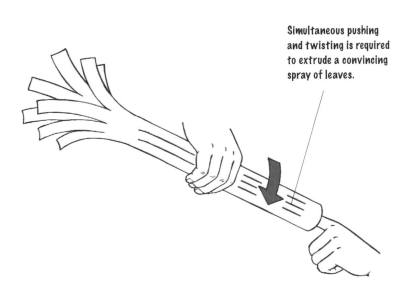

Simultaneous pushing and twisting is required to extrude a convincing spray of leaves.

Anyway, pull out four or five sheets (that's a piece of paper with four pages on it) and tear them in half along the center crease. To start you'll find that the palm tree will work best with eight to ten pages, but with experience you could use more. Take your first single page and roll it up lengthwise. This should give you a nice skinny roll, with a finger-sized space left in the middle. Now take a second sheet and roll it tightly in the same direction around the first. Repeat until you have used all the sheets.

When you have done this, take the scissors and, starting at one end, poke one leg of the scissors into the hole in the middle and then cut down 6 to 8 inches (15 to 20 cm). Repeat this action three to five more times around this end of your newspaper roll. Next, grasping the roll firmly in one hand, poke the index finger of the other hand into the bottom of the roll. While pushing up with the finger, twist the other hand in the direction that will slowly tighten the roll. This forces the inside sheets upward, each one opening out into a fabulous spray. Your admiring audience can even paint them.

Tip: *Works well with the "Homemade volcano" (see pages 58–59) to create a South Seas ambience. It might not hurt to hum the melody of "Hawai'i Aloha" while opening up the palm.*

Juggling

A popular metaphor for modern parenthood rendered real.

DEGREE OF DIFFICULTY

★ ★ ★ ★ ★

(We won't lie.)

APPARATUS

Three good-sized balls of equal diameter (tennis balls work fine).

How to

This is one show turn that works for every youthful audience, from toddler to teen. Yes, we'll be honest, it is hard to learn. But you should be able to do it—if you put in the time. Your dedication will get its due rewards.

Start with one ball. Hold it in your right hand. (Reverse what follows if you are left-handed.) Keep your forearms in front of you and parallel to the floor, and your elbows at your side. The first thing you do is casually toss the ball up—say to yourself "right" as you do so—so that it reaches eye level, and then curves over and drops nicely into your left hand. Try hard not to move your hand up when you catch the ball: let it do the work and come to you. Now toss it back from your left hand to your right, now saying "left" as you do so. Keep doing this for a while, until you can toss the ball effortlessly from your right hand to your left, and back.

Now let's throw a second ball into the mix. Hold this in your left hand. Start by throwing the ball in your right hand. Toss it up, saying "right" to yourself as you do so. At the moment it reaches the top of its arc, and before it starts to fall, toss the left ball up, saying "left" to yourself. You've just freed up your left hand to catch the first ball. You might want to say "catch" to yourself as you catch it, and again when you catch the second ball in your right hand. Practice this until you can get the two balls moving back and forth smoothly. You should have a good rhythm going, of "right, left, catch, catch."

Finally, you are going to add a third ball. To do this you will have one ball in your left hand, and two in your right—one held between your thumb and first two fingers, the other resting in your palm (novices be warned: avoid bowling balls and other outsized crowd-pleasers—master the simple stuff first). Toss the ball held in your right fingers first. Then, as before, when it reaches the top of its arc, toss the left-hand ball up. But now, when the left hand ball reaches the top of its arc, toss the second right-hand ball. To help you, don't forget your silent sequence of chants "Right, left, right," and then "Left, right, left," and so on.

At some point in here you'll probably start to wonder why something as simple as simultaneously raising kids, building a career, looking after elderly parents, and trying to keep the magic in your marriage alive is ever compared to something as complex as having three tennis balls spinning through the air. Despair not. Keep it up and you'll be juggling. Who knows? Eventually you may think nothing of including a unicycle, a chain saw, a bowler hat, and a bent umbrella into your act. At the very least, you could whistle frenetic circus tunes while dazzling the junior set.

We've said it before: don't just perform, teach. Once you've worked it through step by step for yourself, you can show your kids how to do it. They can use it to amuse and, yes, impress their friends. Better, once you have someone else in the house who can juggle you might even want to try your hand at two-person juggling, or "passing." When you start with the two balls in your right hand, instead of throwing the ball up, you toss it across to the other person, at the same time as the other person throws to you. You effortlessly catch their ball in your left hand, and on and on. Next stop: a televised command performance before the shadowy dictator of a former Soviet republic ending in "–stan." The experts say passing works better with clubs (big wooden bowling pins) than balls, but we know what we would rather have smack us in the middle of the forehead.

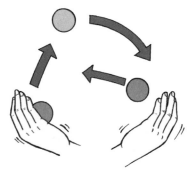

Tip: *Try to keep your hands down. Let the balls fall into them naturally, and avoid moving forward. If the balls seem too complex, some people recommend trying to juggle using three chiffon scarves. You'll be working on the same timing problems but the slower movement of the scarves will give you time to think.*

CHAPTER 4

GAMES AND ACTIVITIES

Making doughnuts

Mom cooks what everyone is supposed to eat; Dad cooks what kids want to eat. This is interactive fun for almost the whole family.

DEGREE OF DIFFICULTY

Beginners should not attempt.

APPARATUS

Cooking oil, a pot or pan, doughnut batter, in-laws in a faraway town.

How to

As Mom pulls away in the car to visit her suitably distant parents, Dad leads the kids to the kitchen. There, he finds the following ingredients:

2 cups (220 g) flour

1/2 cup (115 g) sugar

2 teaspoons baking powder

1 teaspoon salt

1/4 teaspoon ground cinnamon

1/8 teaspoon ground nutmeg

2 tablespoons butter or shortening, softened

1 egg, beaten

1/2 cup (120 ml) milk

oil for deep frying

extra sugar for sprinkling

Combine all the ingredients (except the oil, and the sugar for sprinkling) and mix vigorously into a sticky dough. Then turn the mixture out onto a floured board.

Roll the dough out until it's about 1/3 inches (1 cm or so) thick and leave it to rise for 20 minutes. Then, cut it into strips about 1/3 inches (1.5 cm) wide and 5 inches (12 cm) long, joining up the ends of each strip to form the classic doughnut shape (this is a good bit for the kids to do).

Heat a deep fryer or a frying pan filled with cooking oil to 380°F (195°C). To see if the oil is hot enough, drop a teaspoon of doughnut mix into the oil. If the temperature is right, the oil will bubble and the dough will float. If the dough sinks inertly, wait for the temperature to rise a little more.

Drop in the first doughnuts a few at a time. Turn them in the oil with a fork to ensure even cooking, and remove them carefully when they're a nice golden brown. Leave them to drain on some paper towels for a minute or so, then sprinkle them with sugar. Consume. Repeat.

Warning: Basking in their children's appreciation, some fathers will be tempted to gild the lily. However tempted you are to go for an encore, under no conditions should you bob for a doughnut.

Tip: *Avoid your audience's entreaties to be allowed to consume doughnuts well past bedtime while watching TV.*

Paper boat

Create the classic paper boat with only a modicum of wailing and tooth-gnashing.

DEGREE OF DIFFICULTY
★★★★☆

APPARATUS

A sheet of paper.

How to

Take a sheet of standard paper, such as that used in a laser or inkjet printer. Fold this in half lengthwise, and then unfold it. Now fold it in half widthwise. Lay the paper flat on a table so that the fold is at the top. Take the top left- and right-hand corners and fold them down, so that each corner touches on the center crease left by originally folding the paper lengthwise. You now have two triangles with one long rectangle below them. Fold this up on this side, so that it overlaps the two triangles, and fold the sticking-out corners of the rectangle over the edge of the triangles. Turn the paper over and do the same on the other side with the rectangular strip of paper.

Now you have what looks like a hat. There is a crease running down the middle of this hat on either side.

Put your thumbs inside the hat and under this crease, and tug gently in opposite directions to open out the hat. Pulling it open and flattening it, you now have a diamond shape. Fold up one side of the diamond to make a triangle, and do the same on the other side so that you now have a triangle with each side bisected by a fold.

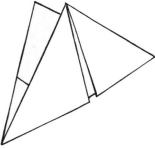

Use your thumbs to pull open the triangle as you did with the hat shape before. Pulling it open and flattening it once more, you now have another diamond shape. Where the left- and right-hand sides of the diamond bisect, pull the two halves open, away from the middle. The triangular mast asserts itself, and a boat is born.

Tip: *A few sheets of paper may have to be sacrificed to get this one right. Wasteful? Just remember: almost all prototypes cost more and take longer to build than expected. Why should yours be any different?*

Storytelling with cards

A clever card trick that works—we still don't understand how.

How to

Here's a card trick with a difference, more story than magic—although it has plenty of that, too. From a deck of cards, take out the aces, jacks, kings, and queens. Now, take one card at random from the deck, and put it facedown upon the table. This is the inn. It doesn't matter what card you pick, this card is just going to sit here for the rest of the story.

Now the story begins. There was once a silly innkeeper who had an inn with four rooms. One night, four workmen came to the inn looking for rooms. Because he had four rooms, the innkeeper decided to put one workman in each room. And with this you take the four jacks and, face up, starting above the card you've picked for the inn and moving clockwise, lay one jack above the inn, one to the right, one below it, and one to the left.

Next, you say, four policemen showed up at the inn, looking for rooms. Thinking for a moment, the innkeeper decided to put one policeman in each room. And with this, you take the aces and, starting at the top, lay one face up on each of the jacks.

Now, no sooner had the innkeeper settled the policemen in their rooms, and made it back down to the front desk when four gentlemen showed up, looking for, you guessed it, rooms for the night. Well, the innkeeper isn't dumb, right? Four gentlemen, four rooms—he knows what to do. He puts a gentleman in each room. And with this, you put one king face up on each of the piles.

At this point, the landlord is feeling pretty tired, but no sooner does he get down to the desk again, when he discovers four ladies standing there, all of whom want a room for the night. Well, the innkeeper knows the drill. He takes the ladies upstairs and puts one in each room. And with this you take the four queens and lay one face up on each of the four piles.

About a minute later, the ladies tear down to the front desk. Are you mad?, they ask him. People can't share rooms like this, all mixed up. Put everyone in a room according to who they are—all the workmen in one room, the policemen in another, the gents in a third, and the ladies in the fourth. With this, pick up each of the piles, turning them facedown and laying each pile on top of the other. Now let your audience cut the cards, as often as they like. When they're done, pick up the cards, and, starting at the top and going around clockwise, distribute them facedown one by one, until you have four piles of four cards. Now flip them over. All the aces will be together, all the kings, all the queens, and all the jacks. Why? It has something to do with sequences.

Tip: *Make especially sure that your audience only cuts the cards, not actively shuffles them, which will break up the sequence and ruin the trick.*

Pub legs

A great car game from the United Kingdom ripe for export across the globe.

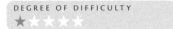

DEGREE OF DIFFICULTY

★☆☆☆☆

APPARATUS

A car, a series of secondary roads, laxer licensing laws, and (most important) one English-speaking liberal constitutional monarchy, located close to, but not actually touching Europe.

How to

Throughout *Dadzooks*, we have taken pains to come up with ideas that are not bound by particular geography. What we have shown you here would work in Slough or Encino, Mississauga, Ontario, or Woolongong, New South Wales. These have truly been the jests and japes of all the English-speaking peoples, a series of tricks and diversions on which it may be said, the sun never sets.

Now, we'd like to throw all of that out of the window. We don't want to, but Pub Legs is just too good a game to pass up. Britons can play it whenever they want, and others can pick it up should they have cause to visit Albion's sceptered isle. Our fond hope, too, is that others will see how the game works, and adapt it to suit their own local conditions. If nothing else, it should appeal to any junior Anglophiles; those with a fondness for Harry Potter, say.

Waffling out of the way, here's how it works. This is a smaller road sort of game; it won't work on big highways (what are known in the United Kingdom as motorways). You want smaller country roads, and city streets. Designate one child and tell them their job is to look out for pub names, and to keep a running tally of the number of legs suggested by the name. For example, if you see "The Drunken Merchant Banker," that counts as two legs. If you then drive past "The Happy Football Hooligan," that counts as two more. Whoever is it just keeps adding up the legs in the names—until you hit a name with no legs in it, for example, "The Bell" or "The Wheat Sheaf." At that point, they are out, and someone else takes their turn to start counting. A running total is kept and at the end of the trip, whoever has the greatest number of legs, wins.

It is possible to rack up quite gargantuan scores—for example, near Windsor just outside London there used to be a pub called "The Army and Navy," which gave you an instantaneous 250,000 legs. With its astronomical scores and strange outs, pub legs resembles nothing so much as cricket. Its degree of arbitrariness (losing your turn has nothing to do with how well you played or how clever you are, it comes down purely to caprice) also exposes children to the fundamentally unfair, some might even say, tragic, nature of life. This inherent unfairness may also remind many of us why our ancestors left the Old World in the first place. Whatever, pub legs is one of those fine English pastimes, like fives or the Eton wall game, that deserve to be better known.

 Tip: *Spice things up by declaring any names with non-leg body parts (say, "The Duke's Head") as instant outs.*

Gridiron and tongs

A homemade trick with wire loops, and a bit of a twist.

DEGREE OF DIFFICULTY
★ ★ ★ ★ ☆

APPARATUS

Two pieces of wire—any kind, although plastic covered electrical wire works best.

How to

Around 1900, wire puzzles were very much in vogue, and hundreds of them were dreamed up. They are still a favorite of mathematicians and other such brainy folk, who like them because they illustrate valuable lessons about . . . uh, topology. We have no idea what topology is and neither, probably, do you. That aside, this is an interesting puzzle to make and explain—and it actually isn't all that hard.

The puzzle consists of two parts. First, there's the gridiron, which is the vaguely mazelike square construction. Looking at the diagram, you'll notice that one end of the gridiron wire is left free, while the other end is looped very broadly around the gridiron itself. The second piece is the tongs, which feature a long, narrow opening, some twists, and then two fanciful curlicues at the ends.

When you have made these two shapes—pliers might be helpful— and made sure the tongs are firmly attached to the gridiron, you hand it to your audience and ask them to remove the tongs from the gridiron without bending or twisting it or undoing the large loop in the gridiron. Even though the gridiron is open at one end, you'll never be able to maneuver the tongs so that they just come off. But let your audience discover this for themselves. They might catch on to what they need to do, or they might not.

The secret lies in thinking a little outside the box. Thread the tongs through the small loop in the end of the girdiron. Pass the long loop through first, then maneuver the curlicues in the end around and through one at a time. It won't look, at first glance, as if they will make it, but they will.

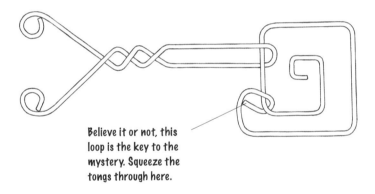

Believe it or not, this loop is the key to the mystery. Squeeze the tongs through here.

Tip: *The key to making the trick properly challenging is to make the loop on the gridiron the same general width as the loop on the tongs. Too small, and the trick becomes impossible; too big, and the trick becomes too obvious.*

"Golden Hair"

A sure-fire ghost story, guaranteed to thrill pre-teens at bedtime.

DEGREE OF DIFFICULTY
★★★★☆

APPARATUS

None.

How to

Every dad needs a good ghost story. Here is one originally from Corsica, suggested by Canadian storyteller Lorne Brown.

There once was a beautiful blonde girl known as Golden Hair. In a castle overlooking Golden Hair's village lived the wicked Count Renaldo, who loved her golden hair. He wanted to marry Golden Hair. Golden Hair's mother was happy because it meant her little daughter would become a countess. And Golden Hair's father felt Count Renaldo could do whatever he wanted with her as long as he paid him a big bag of money. But Golden Hair really loved a peasant lad called Pietro. The count knew this, and so he hatched a plot. One night, the wicked count lay in wait for Pietro. As Pietro walked by, Count Renaldo jumped out, swinging his sword wildly. Pietro was taken by surprise and the count almost got him, but in the terrific fight, Pietro killed him with his hunting knife. Now Pietro was in trouble because the count had a lot of followers. He had to escape to a far-off land. But before he left, he promised Golden Hair he would return someday.

Several years pass. One day Golden Hair is at the market. It's crowded that day, and as she pushes her way from stall to stall, a small child slips through the crush and hands her a letter. Golden Hair reads the letter. It's from Pietro. He says he's going to come for her that very night between the hours of midnight and rooster-crow. Wait for me, he tells her—he'll carry her away on his horse.

That night, Golden Hair waits by her window, excited. At midnight a horse and rider materialize and the rider whispers up to her, "Come down now, I'll take you away." She steals downstairs quietly, so her parents don't hear, and slips out the door. It's dark and the rider is cloaked in a robe. He reaches down and lifts her up on the back of his horse and away they gallop.

They travel through the night, and to Golden Hair it seems as if they are riding through every country in the world. She looks one way and she sees the pyramids of Egypt. A little later, she looks the other way, and they are passing the Great Wall of China. On and on they ride. They pass a graveyard and a voice calls out: "Look, a youth riding with his maid! But aren't you afraid, maiden? Aren't you afraid?"

"What have I got to be afraid of?" Golden Hair calls back. "I'm riding with my Pietro."

They pass another graveyard and another voice comes out from among the tombstones: "Look! A youth riding with a maiden. Aren't you afraid, maiden, to be riding with the dead?"

"I'm not riding with the dead," she calls, "I'm riding with my Pietro."

But then the rider turns around. It's not Pietro, it's the dead, very dead and decayed, Count Renaldo. Leering at her, he says, "You spurned me in life, but I will have you in death!" And on and on they gallop, ever faster and faster toward the end of the world. There, the great iron gates of the kingdom of the dead are slowly opening to receive them. "Help me," she begs the count's horse. "Stop, oh, please stop!" but it keeps on galloping.

Luckily, at that very moment, Pietro is riding toward Golden Hair's village. He hears the cry. It's her! Quickly, he turns his horse and chases after her. The count has a headstart but Pietro is hot on his heels, spurring his horse on through the night. Slowly he gains on them. He's just inches behind. Golden Hair tries to jump off, but the dead count grabs her by her golden hair and won't let go. Pietro catches up just as the iron gates to the kingdom of the dead are opening wide. He reaches out with his hunting knife and cuts through the girl's golden hair, grabbing her just at the moment when Count Renaldo and his horse rush through the gateway. The iron gates slam behind them with a great clang. Count Renaldo has only her golden hair—but that's all he ever really loved. Pietro has Golden Hair and she has him. Holding her close to him, Pietro takes her away to their new home in a distant land, where they live out their lives in great happiness.

Tip: *When it comes to storytelling, Lorne Brown suggests keeping it straight. Don't mumble in a monotone, but avoid gestures and overly dramatic voices. We suggest this possible variation to increase the story's immediacy: As you reach the end of the story, after the lines "live out their lives in great happiness," casually add the line "until one day Count Ronaldo returned"—and this is your cue to get ready to yell—"and grabbed her!" while simultaneously seizing your listener to good effect.*

There's one

An open ended, and seemingly inexhaustible, car game.

DEGREE OF DIFFICULTY
★★★★★

APPARATUS

None.

How to

This is a guessing game that any observant kid can enjoy, though very small ones may have trouble with it, either through lack of words or because their child safety seat cramps their ability to see what's going on. Anyway, here's how it works. You, Dad, are it, first. Pick something by or on the road—say, a highway sign or a red Volkswagen. Tell the kids that you have an object in mind, and every time you pass or see one, you'll say, "There's one." You remain it until one of your passengers guesses what the mystery object is. Then it's their go. It is the ultimate boredom reliever, with no real winners or losers, and lasts as long as people want.

Tip: *Avoid choosing anything too abstract—"Man's inhumanity to man," say. Don't choose anything so common as to be obvious, or so rare that players can never figure it out. Picking a pine tree just as you enter the Mojave Desert may seem clever, but your kids are going to be dismayed, perhaps even frightened, to see Dad fall silent for days.*

Flip book

Homemade cinematic magic created from the very barest essentials.

DEGREE OF DIFFICULTY
★★☆☆☆

APPARATUS
A paperclip, and some index cards or other thin cardboard.

How to

This is not so much a trick to show off, as a skill to teach. (It was, we believe, the venerable sage Confucius who said, "Make a child a flip book and you amuse him for about ten seconds; teach a child to make them and amuse him for, if not a lifetime, certainly rather longer.") And as making flip books can be somewhat time-consuming, after you impart your knowledge you will be free to nap, watch TV, and undertake other such important activities. The first thing you'll need is a supply of light card. Classic index cards would be a good choice, but if you can't find them any quantity of equally flimsy cardstock would work fine. With index cards, start by cutting them widthwise to make strips about an inch (2.5 cm) across. You should be able to get five such strips out of one index card. Once you've got a number of these, the real work begins. To keep it easy, let's make our first flip book story something very simple—just a stick figure running. On the first index-card strip, draw a stick figure with his legs wide apart as if he were belting along. Then move this strip up, and use our man as a reference for the second strip, where you show your character with his legs in a slightly different spot. Then move up the second strip and use the newly positioned character as a reference while you make the third, and on and on. When you have a bunch of these, gather them up, make sure that the outer edges of your card pieces (on the side of the image) are more or less even for ease of riffling, and clip the lot together at the other end with a paper or bulldog clip. Now flick through the pages with your thumb and behold—Dad is a regular Martin Scorsese.

Tip: *Generally, the greater the number of separate images, the more effective the flip book—which is another reason to have the kids working on it directly.*

Cool paper plane

A slightly different take on the ever-popular paper airplane.

DEGREE OF DIFFICULTY
★★★★☆

APPARATUS

A sheet of standard note paper, lined or unlined.

How to

Most kids can create a paper airplane of their own, but this is a much fancier version, requiring a certain degree of work.

Start with any standard sheet of paper—the kind used in a regular printer works fine. First, turn the paper sideways, so that it is wider than it is tall. Take the upper left-hand corner, and fold it down so that the left-hand edge meets the bottom edge. You'll see a strip about an inch wide to the right of the folded over part. Cut or tear this off (cutting is better), and put it aside—we'll want it later on. For now, though, you have a square to work with.

Now let's get busy folding. Let's call the upper left- and right-hand corners A, the bottom left- and right-hand corners, B. We want to fold these down so that A and B meet. But first we are going to create two diagonal creases, running from corner to corner. These are lines C. After you have made these creases, fold the paper in half, so that A meets B. Fold this first one way, toward you, and then fold it along this line the other way. We're going to call the points on either end of this crease in the paper D. Now it gets complex. While folding A over to B, fold inward along the diagonal creases C so that the two points D meet.

What you should have is a small triangle with the rest of the paper folded in and under.

Lying this flat, with the base of the triangle at the top and the point at the bottom, take the two upper corners and fold them down to the point. This gives you a diamond shape. This may not seem readily useful, but be patient. You'll notice that folding down the upper edges has created a sort of a seam right in the middle. Now, take the upper edges of the diamond and fold them down in to this center seam. After that, take the bottom halves of the diamond and fold them into the center seam, refolding the top folds so that they overlap the bottom folds and now come to a point that protrudes about an inch behind the original tip of the diamond. Now we refold the line we made that bisected the sides of the diamond, turning the first point under but leaving the second protruding. This is now the nose of our aircraft, which protrudes past the blunt leading edge of the wing. At this point we take the plane and fold it up in half so that the two wing tips meet. Then unfold it. This gives the wings a slight dihedral shape. Finally we take the strip of paper we cut off at the beginning. Fold it in half lengthwise, and tuck it in to give the plane a tail for added stability. A thing of beauty.

Tip: Be patient. The only way we could do this was by breathing into a paper bag a few times. Sharp folds help, as does starting with a large piece of paper. If it seems difficult, remember the pioneers of aviation and count yourself lucky.

Four good riddles

Build supple minds through these popular brainteasers.

How to

Modern parents are nothing if not pragmatic. When they consider a TV show, a new toy, or even a potential friend for their child, all they want to know is, Will this benefit my child in the battleground that is their future life? Today it's all about the right school, the right university, and ultimately the right job. And no doubt some of you, as you work your way through this book's instructions on homemade volcanoes, paper airplanes, and Mentos explosions, are probably wondering, How will this help little Shipley or Tamsin? Well, you may rest assured. Here are four riddles that are specially designed to promote mental fortitude, transmuting simple childish wonder, the sort of thing that delights in a butterfly or a sunbeam, say, into diamond-hard, diamond-brilliant intellect, of the sort that will allow your child to someday trade derivatives—while, with a bit of luck, avoiding any threat of criminal prosecution. And all disguised as innocuous fun.

Riddle No. 1

Q. What is the beginning of eternity, the end of time and space, the beginning of every end, and the end of every place?

A. Sounds profound, doesn't it? Could it be a black hole? Or one of those weird time-space portals that they were always coming across on the original *Star Trek* show? Actually, it's much, much simpler. The answer is the letter e.

Riddle No. 2

Q. What goes on four legs in the morning, on two legs at noon, and on three legs in the evening?

A. A man—as a baby he crawls on the floor, as a grown man he walks upright, and then when he is old he needs a cane.

Tip: *This was the famous riddle of the Greek Sphinx, who beseiged the city of Thebes. She posed it to all passers-by, and if you got it wrong, you were history. Apparently, Oedipus (yes, the Oedipus) was the first person to guess it correctly, whereupon the Sphinx ceased to exist. We don't put much stock in ancient legends, but if your young lad manages to get this one right, you might want to think about what happened to Oedipus's Dad—and Mom, for that matter. Nothing heavy-handed of course, but definitely keep an eye on the young fellow.*

Riddle No. 3

Q. As I was going to St. Ives, I met a man with seven wives
Each wife had seven sacks, each sack had seven cats,
Each cat had seven kits. Kits, cats, sacks, and wives,
How many were going to St. Ives?

A. Again this one looks like murder, and the reaction of most
people, even adults, is to start calculating (Hmm, seven wives
times seven cats, uh . . .). In fact, the answer is one. One person,
the narrator, was going to St. Ives. He or she met all these
wives, cats, kits, and so on because they were going in the
opposite direction.

Riddle No. 4

This is one of the most famous of modern riddles. It is also quite
complicated. But it can be solved, by older children at least. In
fact, they may do better at it than adults whose brains are
clogged with the dross of decades of school and work. If they
don't get it at first, you can always explain it to them, and then
they can use it on their friends.

All right, here's how it works. There is a train, traveling
between Chicago and Detroit, and on this train there is an
engineer, a fireman (this is an old-fashioned train), and a
brakeman. One of them is named Mr. Smith, one of them is
named Mr. Jones, and one of them is named Mr. Robinson. By an
amazing coincidence, there are three passengers on the train with
exactly the same names. Now here are the clues. Have your
audience listen to them quite carefully because each one of them
is important.

1. Mr. Robinson lives in Detroit.

2. The brakeman lives exactly halfway between Chicago and Detroit.

3. Mr. Jones earns exactly $20,000 per year.

4. The brakeman's nearest neighbor, one of the passengers, earns exactly three times as much as the brakeman.

5. Smith beats the fireman in billiards.

6. The passenger whose name is the same as the brakeman's lives in Chicago.

Who is the engineer?

First of all, we know that Mr. Robinson lives in Detroit, but the brakeman lives halfway between Detroit and Chicago. So the brakeman's name is either Smith or Jones. Then we are told that Mr. Jones earns $20,000 a year, but that the brakeman's nearest neighbor earns exactly three times as much as the brakeman. $20,000 cannot be divided exactly by three, so Mr. Jones is not the brakeman's neighbor. It would have to be Smith. Then we are told that Smith beat the fireman at billiards. Whether Smith is a passenger or a crew member doesn't matter: we know that the fireman cannot be called Smith. Then we are told that the passenger with the same name as the brakeman lives in Chicago. Well, we know it's not Robinson and we know it's not Smith, so the brakeman is named Jones. The fireman who cannot be Smith and now cannot be Jones must be Robinson. We've got Jones, we've got Robinson, so the engineer can only be Smith.

Homemade kite

Watch a child's eyes grow wide with wonder when Dad recycles the detritus of our industrial society—or something like that.

DEGREE OF DIFFICULTY
★★★☆

APPARATUS

Thin string, tape, sticks, a trash bag.

How to

Yes, we know you can buy a kite. Yes, we know you're hopeless when it comes to making things. But this is one kite even the most hopeless Dad should be able to make. Let's start with a

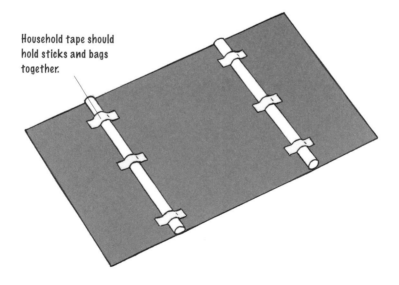

Household tape should hold sticks and bags together.

garbage bag, ideally a large one, at least 32 by 18 inches (80 by 45 cm). We only need one side of the bag, so cut along the seams and put one half aside. You'll need this in a moment. Lay the other half flat, so that it is wider than it is high. Fold in the outer edges, and mark where the creases are. You are going to tape two struts running from one side to the other along these lines.

The struts can be made of pretty well anything—cardboard, strips of plastic, even light bamboo stakes—but they must be (a) light and (b) strong. Now, measure down the strut one third of its length and make a mark. Taking the upper left-hand corner of your bag, fold it down to this spot. Repeat on the upper right-hand side. Cut along these folds with your scissors. Then, taking the bottom two corners, fold them in on a diagonal line starting

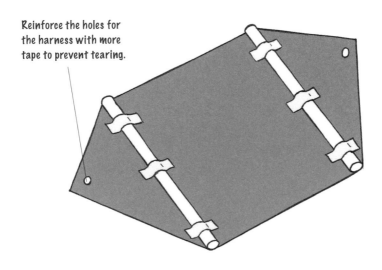

Reinforce the holes for the harness with more tape to prevent tearing.

at the top diagonal line and running down to the very bottom of the strut. Do this on the other side as well. You now have what looks like a traditional kite with a blocky extra section in the middle. Measuring a little under 1 inch (2.5 cm) in from either point, put down a piece of sticky tape, and then poke a hole through it. This is going to hold the harness. Attach a very thin line (something nylon would be good) about 8 feet (2.5 m) long to each hole, then tie them together to a single piece of line that you will use to control the kite.

Your kite will also need a tail. Forget the classic bows: this kite uses a loop tail—a strip of trash bag (why not? You have plenty) about 6 feet (2 m) long and about 1.5 inches (2 cm) wide that loops down from one strut and joins up to the other. This provides stability. If you want to fly this kite in high winds, you might consider cutting round holes a couple of inches wide in the lower part of the central section, to stop it from tearing apart.

You may not be aware of it, but kites have a long and glorious history. It was likely the Chinese who invented them about three thousand years ago. (Please, we're talking, stop waving your hand.) From there, they spread out all across the Old World. And while today they are just toys (Yeah, yeah, in a minute), once upon a time they were serious tools in the pursuit of scientific knowledge. Benjamin Franklin flew a kite with a key suspended from it during a thunder storm to prove that lightning was electricity. And those great aviation pioneers the Wright Brothers made a lot of the early discoveries that would help them build the first working aircraft by flying kite—

Oh, never mind . . .

The use of trash bags is called recycling in action (not Dad being cheap.)

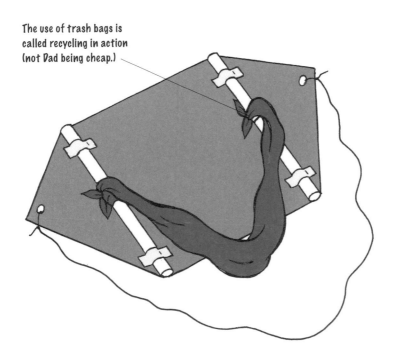

Tip: *After building a kite comes flying one. This takes two. One of you stays put and pays out the line, while the other (Dad is good for this) walks about 30 feet (9 m) away, and holds up the kite so that the wind catches it. Your hearts will soar as the kite gains its freedom and wafts heavenward. Yeah, well, that's the theory.*

ScheheraDad

Father weaves 1,001 nights of custom-tailored story.

DEGREE OF DIFFICULTY

★★★★☆

APPARATUS
A decent memory combined with a degree of stoicism.

How to

Reading to your kids is great and reminiscing about your own childhood is wonderful, too. But there is one more form of storytelling that anyone who was ever its recipient as a child remembers for the rest of their lives: a story made up by Dad and told just for them. Probably it wasn't the best story in the world—go back and look at it now and you'd probably notice yawning logical inconsistencies and plenty of loose threads (Why did the Jolly June Bugs family have slurred voices after the office party? And what the hell was so scary about the Escalator of Doom?)—but it was theirs and theirs alone. For most of us, who can't even come up with a plausible story when we want to take a day off work, this may seem hard, but by breaking it down into small steps, anyone can do this.

1. Create a character

The key here is to know your audience. Is it two girls, eight and 10? Then a nine-year-old girl is a good choice for a heroine. Trying to entertain a seven-year-old boy? Then a small boy will do fine. The key to remember is that your audience will do a lot of the work for you. You don't have to create every detail—just mention that he or she lives at home, or had red hair, and you have fleshed out the hero enough for your audience to do the rest.

2. The turnaround

Read enough fairy tales or study enough of those books that promise to turn you into a screenwriter, and you'll quickly see that what really gets the story going is one incident. Think of *Alice in Wonderland*. She's sitting outside with her sister, who is reading an incredibly dull book. Bored, Alice looks around and spies a white rabbit hopping by muttering, "I'm late, I'm late." That gets Alice interested and off she goes. Your story can do something similar. Have the hero or heroine headed to school, or going to the store, or going on holidays, when something—and it can pretty well be anything—happens.

3. Challenges and responses

When discussing TV shows and movies, you sometimes hear people talk about their three-act structure. The turnaround above is what starts the second act. From here, your story starts to take on a life of its own. Essentially, what you need to do is create problems or challenges that the hero has to confront and overcome. Locked doors with no keys, dragons, and ruinous tax bills are all excellent examples of such challenges. Keep tossing them in and having the hero overcome them. If your storytelling is a nightly affair, take a tip from the old-fashioned silent films like *The Perils of Pauline*: if your hero gets away from the dragon by jumping into the river, he or she should see a waterfall directly ahead. But how they get out of it is a story for another night.

Cliffhangers build suspense, and give you an entire day to figure out how to get your characters out of trouble. Don't be afraid to borrow or recycle old stories. Hollywood does it all the time—why shouldn't you?

One of the best things about telling a children's story is that it never has to end. You have a first act and a second, but you don't have to worry about a third. Anthony Powell or Marcel Proust had to rack their brains to figure out how to tie up the loose ends when they wanted to wind up their multivolume epics, but you just keep going—there is always another eerie castle, another enchanted forest, another ogre with issues. Ultimately the kids will grow up and move away. And if they never leave, sooner or later they'll put you into a home—problem solved.

Tip: *Don't worry too much about detail. Your audience should be doing most of the imaginative heavy lifting. If your heroine is running through a dark forest, leave it at that or, at most, make it a dark pine forest. Leave the fetishistic description to Nicholson Baker. And learn to depend on the threes. For some reason, everything in fairy tales and folk stories seems to revolve around repetitions of three: three great dogs, three doors, three beautiful princesses. Embrace this rule, and avoid the temptation, if in a hurry, to try to get by with only two doors, two great dogs, or two princesses.*

Poor dead mice

Looks like a hardware problem but IT Dad is on the scene.

DEGREE OF DIFFICULTY
★ ☆ ☆ ☆ ☆

APPARATUS

A piece of tape, small enough to conceal.

How to

Every kid on the planet knows more about the computer, the web, and where to find the stuff you're not supposed to see than their father. When it comes to the computer you are a very old dog to be learning tricks let alone performing them. But here is a simple practical joke that you can perform and then pass on.

Take the computer's mouse and place a small piece of tape over the roller ball or the red optical sensor. When your kid comes to the computer, they will be baffled. The mouse is connected, but the cursor won't move. Feign concern, squint at the screen, then show them what you've done. This is one joke they can play on their friends. Suggest they do that—or better yet, go out and play. It's too nice a day to be sitting inside at a computer.

Now, how the heck do you find those pics of Lindsay Lohan?

Tip: *Try some techspeak: "Maybe a problem with the shunt drive" or "the woberon probably needs its fritillary regigged."*

"When I was a lad . . ."

Dad's memories, suitably sepia-tinted for
a new generation.

DEGREE OF DIFFICULTY
★★★☆☆

APPARATUS

None. Well, your own
memories and a fairly simple
technique.

How to

Most of us can still remember the stories our parents or grandparents used to tell about their childhoods: up every morning at
three; walking to school uphill both ways through the sleet and
snow; a lump of suet for lunch; a simple, smooth stone as a
birthday present. Happy? Ahh, those were the days.

But when it comes to our own lives, our tales by and large
don't seem to have the same oomph. "If you had even one Duran
Duran T-shirt," you imagine telling your wide-eyed kids, "you were
grateful." That's if you can really pick out anything memorable in
the first place. For a lot of us, it's all now just an undifferentiated
blur. The old joke about the sixties (that if you can remember
them, you weren't there) seems all too fitting applied to our
childhood experiences of the seventies, eighties, and nineties.

Don't worry, you do have stories and your kids will find them
incredible. Here's a tip from Lorne Brown, a professional storyteller,
that should help. However much the world has changed, there is
at least one thing your kids do that you did as well: you went to
school. Start with that. Think of your week and their week. How
did you get to school? Did you walk? Now, how do they get

there? When you had lunch, what food did you have? What did you study? What do your kids study now? When you watched TV, what did you watch and how many channels were there? What clothes did you wear? Which ones did you really covet?

As you go on, you'll start to spot more and more differences between your childhood and theirs. Don't be worried that your memories won't seem astounding. You should keep in mind that everything you are telling them is completely new to them. Seemingly neutral comments—"We walked to school," "We didn't have bottled water, we just drank what came out of the faucet," or "Sushi? When I was your age, I'd never seen raw fish, much less eaten it"—will conjure up a world as strange to them as life on Mars. Your tales of retroactively realized youthful hardship will garner you new-found respect in the eyes of your children.

Tip: *Generally, Brown says, there is no need to exaggerate. What you are telling them straight will already seem so strange that you won't need to embellish. That said, a slight degree of hyperbole is allowed—nay, encouraged. When giving distances, always go for the greatest possible estimate. When talking about, say, walking to school in winter, the very coldest temperature ever can stand in for every day. When discussing money, the smallest amount ever paid for something (a CD, say) should be cited as completely typical.*